THE POLITICS OF
EARLY OLD ENGLISH
SOUND CHANGE

QUANTITATIVE ANALYSES OF LINGUISTIC STRUCTURE

Under the general editorship of

William Labov
University of Pennsylvania

David Sankoff
Centre de Recherches Mathematique

THE POLITICS OF EARLY OLD ENGLISH SOUND CHANGE

Thomas E. Toon

Department of English Language and Literature
University of Michigan
Ann Arbor, Michigan

ACADEMIC PRESS
A Subsidiary of Harcourt Brace Jovanovich, Publishers
New York   London
Paris   San Diego   San Francisco   São Paulo   Sydney   Tokyo   Toronto

ACADEMIC PRESS, INC.
111 Fifth Avenue, New York, New York 10003

United Kingdom Edition published by
ACADEMIC PRESS, INC. (LONDON) LTD.
24/28 Oval Road, London NW1   7DX

Library of Congress Cataloging in Publication Data

Toon, Thomas E.
    The politics of early Old English sound change.

    (Quantitative analysis of linguistic structure series)
    Bibliography: p.
    Includes index.
    1. Anglo-Saxon language--Phonology. 2. Anglo-Saxon
language--Dialects--Phonology. 3. Anglo-Saxon language--
Variation. 4. Anglo-Saxons--Kings and rulers. I. Title.
II. Series.
PE140.T66   1982   429'.15   82-8864
ISBN 0-12-694980-8   AACR2

PRINTED IN THE UNITED STATES OF AMERICA

83 84 85 86   9 8 7 6 5 4 3 2 1

DEDICATION

Eadwine

Forþon wat se þe sceal   his winedryhtnes
leofes larcwidum   longe forþolian,
ðonne sorg ond slæp   somod ætgædre
earmne anhogan   oft gebindað.
Þinceð him on mode   þæt he his mondryhten
clyppe ond cysse,   ond on cneo lecge
honda ond heafod,   swa he hwilum ær
in geardagum   giefstolas breac.

To Edwin

Anyone who has suffered losing the kind counsel
of his beloved lord and friend can understand
how the forlorn man now alone imagines,
when bound by sleep and sorrow together,
that he embraces and kisses his mentor,
lays head and hands on his knee,
as in times gone when he had so often
enjoyed his friend's openhanded giftgiving.

CONTENTS

Contents

2
RECONSTITUTING THE SOUNDS OF OLD ENGLISH

3
POLITICS AND LANGUAGE CHANGE

4
CONSPIRACY AND COMPETITION IN
THE IMPLEMENTATION OF LANGUAGE CHANGE

Contents

5
VARIATION AND CHANGE IN MERCIAN OLD ENGLISH

6
THE STUDY OF EARLY OLD ENGLISH
SOUND CHANGE IN PROGRESS

PREFACE

The subject of literacy has recently developed into a major cross-disciplinary concern in contemporary humanities and social science. The inquiry began with the early ethnographies that documented the profound effects of the written word upon the structure of previously nonliterate cultures. Goody and Watt[1] extended the work to include speculation on the consequences of alphabetic literacy on oral cultures; Eisenstein,[2] Graff,[3] and Lockridge[4] focused the attention of historians on the role that literacy played in the de-

[1] Jack Goody and Ian Watt, "The Consequences of Literacy," in Jack Goody, ed., *Literacy in Traditional Societies* (Cambridge: Cambridge University Press, 1968), pp. 27–68.

[2] Elizabeth L. Eisenstein, *The Printing Press as an Agent of Change* (Cambridge: Cambridge University Press, 1979).

[3] Harvey J. Graff, *The Literacy Myth* (New York: Academic Press, 1979); and Harvey J. Graff, ed., *Literacy and Social Development in the West* (Cambridge: Cambridge University Press, 1981).

[4] Kenneth Lockridge, *Literacy in Colonial New England* (New York: Norton, 1974).

velopment of Western society; Ong[5] has grappled with the ways in which the ever present *word* has influenced Western modes of thought. Within the intellectual climate created by such wide-ranging inquiry, this book examines the period during which the Germanic conquerors of Britain became an English nation, when an oral culture became exposed to the literate traditions of the classical world. The result, of course, was the beginnings of literacy as we know it—the literate tradition of Western Europe whose effects on oral cultures, on Western social development, and on our intellectual make-up we are just beginning to understand. For thirteen hundred years, we speakers of English have been writers of English as well; the world is different because of it. The recent analysis of the consequences of literacy began with the study of oral cultures confronted by European literacy. We now turn to the source to reexamine the original confrontation between preliterate Anglo-Saxons and Latin learning, an event that culminated in the literate tradition within which the inquiry itself is conducted.

Thirteen hundred years of nearly continuous textual documentation also make privileged the position English holds among the world's languages for the study of the processes of linguistic variation and change. The topic of this book is a traditional one—the dialects of English during the early Anglo-Saxon period (A.D. 700–850). However, the work offered here presents an unusual, and until recently an impossible, treatment of the subject. This book claims to be nothing less than a study of the progress of sound changes that we know to have been completed more than a thousand years ago. The methodology that makes such research possible is one that has emerged from the study of ongoing change in contemporary social dialects—the quantitative analysis of linguistic structures. That one is able, as Labov reminds us, to use the present to explain the past means that it is possible to derive startlingly fresh interpretations from the traditional data.

[5] Walter J. Ong, *The Presence of the Word* (New Haven: Yale University Press, 1967); and *Interfaces of the Word* (Ithaca: Cornell University Press, 1977).

Preface

The data of this study consist of the first attempts by anyone to write the English language. The authors of those experiments were native Anglo-Saxons, almost certainly members of religious communities, who had been trained in reading and writing Latin. Before these efforts, Latin had been the exclusive vehicle of literacy in Western Europe, and it continued to be the main vehicle of literate expression for several centuries. That means, among other things, that Christianity and literacy were nearly coterminous. Early English attempts at vernacular literacy were at first limited to a word or phrase written (or sometimes scratched with a sharp point) into a Latin manuscript of a religious text. As that practice became more common, glossaries were compiled and complete interlinear glosses to Bibles and Psalters were added to Latin texts. Scribes soon were employed by kings to make permanent records, and before long kings found it useful to have their own *scriptoria*, that is, cadres of professional writers. With official recognition and support of vernacular literacy, the writing of English flourished. It is impossible to know just how many English documents (or Latin documents containing Old English) were produced between A.D. 700 and 850, since so many Anglo-Saxon cultural artifacts were destroyed by the marauding Norse invaders of the tenth century. Only four extended texts, numerous fragments, and some 35 official documents escaped destruction. The corpus of data treated here is the complete record—drawn from sundry printed editions, checked word by word against the original manuscripts, and reproduced in its entirety. Full explanations of the various sources and complete bibliographic descriptions contextualize the data for nonspecialists.

Audience has been the overriding concern in the recasting of this study in its final form. Because the early Anglo-Saxon manuscripts are the major source of information about that period, these texts have been studied by scholars in a number of disciplines. Unfortunately, art historians, political historians, paleographers, Latinists, Anglo-Saxonists, and linguists have carried on their separate inquiries with very little interdisciplinary communication. It is not surprising that they have come to radically different conclusions about the origin, nature, dating, political status, etc. of the early texts. The eighth-century Latin text of the *Vespasian Psalter (British Museum Cotton Vespasian A. 1),* for example, has been assigned a Canterbury provenience mostly on the basis of the opinions of art historians. The assumed Kentish (southeastern) origin has prompted some Old English dialectologists to argue as well for a Canterbury provenience of the later interlinear vernacular gloss, whereas most regional dialectologists argue that the gloss was most probably written in Mercia (West Midlands). Philologists have dated the gloss ca. A.D. 875, but paleographers have noted orthographic features that are peculiar to Mercian charters but that disappeared from contemporary charters by A.D. 830. The political, social, and religious structures of early England have been all but ignored. In the present study, however, the need for an essentially new interpretive context for analysis of linguistic variation has resulted in a cross-disciplinary study that must be readable for a wide range of scholarly audiences. The focus of this work is linguistic, but I have avoided unmotivated formalisms. The analytic tools employed (variable rules, implicational hierarchies, and the like) have been chosen because they are powerful descriptive, interpretive, and predictive devices for demonstrating patterns in variation.

The variation in the first English texts was accurately recorded by the neogrammarian philologists who began the modern study of historical linguistics, but its linguistic, political, and social significance has gone unnoticed. The present study, by describing and contextualizing the nature of the constraints on "free variation," demonstrates that the texts represent various stages in the chronological development of Old English, thus allowing a merger of diachronic and synchronic perspectives. The investigation correlates the gradual appearance of Mercian orthographic and linguistic features with the solidification of Mercian political supremacy. Since it traces the political, as well as the phonological and lexical, diffusion of non-Northumbrian, non-Kentish, and non-West Saxon linguistic developments during a period of Mercian dominance, this book argues that the linguistic variation produced in this historical context ought not to be limited to a strictly geographical interpretation. What emerges is a sketch of structured heterogeneity and change in a viable speech community under the influence of Mercian overlords.

The argument enables an expansion of the focus of linguistic description. It claims to go beyond an adequate description of what Old English *was* to include aspects of what Anglo-Saxons *did* politically and socially with their language. This study presents evidence from the earliest records of the influence of literacy on the development of the English language, and of the role of written language in the development and maintenance of social structure.

ACKNOWLEDGMENTS

I would like to thank the many who have aided me in the progress and completion of this book: Sherman M. Kuhn kindled and sustained my interest in Mercian varieties of Old English and has continued to insist that I strive for the same rigor that typifies his work; James W. Downer has been himself, which includes being a perennial source of linguistic good sense; Jay L. Robinson, Michael P. Clark, and several anonymous readers have been generous in their friendly and penetrating criticism of earlier drafts. Bernard Van't Hul drew the initials that adorn the chapter openings.

It is a pleasure to acknowledge my debt to the following persons and institutions:

To the University of Michigan Department of English and Horace H. Rackham School of Graduate Studies, who provided me with grants to undertake this research and to prepare this manuscript.

To the librarians of the Vatican Library, the Epinal Bibliotheque Municipale, the Erfurt Wissenschaftliche Allgemeinbibliothek, Bibliotheek der Rijksuniversiteit te Leiden, Canterbury Cathedral Archives and Library, Durham Cathedral Library, Cambridge University Library, the Parker Library of Corpus Christi College Cambridge, The British Museum, and The Pierpont Morgan Library, all of whom made the manuscripts in their collections available for my use.

To the President and Fellows of Clare Hall, Cambridge, for their generous hospitality during my stay there.

Above all, I thank my wife.

THE POLITICS OF
EARLY OLD ENGLISH
SOUND CHANGE

INTRODUCTION

ITTLE is known for certain about the migration of the continental Germanic tribes to their new British homeland, but a few hundred years after the conquest there is a comparative flood of information. That remarkable change suggests that the early Anglo-Saxon period was one of cataclysmic transitions. A preliterate people had conquered a new land and had established there a new social order. They came as warring bands of tribesmen with few interests beyond survival and personal glory in battle. By Bede's time, they could already think of themselves as an English nation of distinctly English cultural, social, and political achievements. Members of a culture as pervasively literate as our own need to be reminded of the magnitude of that change. In oral societies, culture and history reside exclusively in memory; social and political structures depend entirely upon present and immediate balances of power. Spoken agreements are valid only as long as those who spoke them choose to remember them; material possessions are limited to what an individual can grasp and defend. Literacy makes possible a past independent of memory. Written agreements outlive convenience and *document* ownership; bookkeeping makes possible more complex administrative structures; a king can make a permanent ally by granting a privilege for all time in a written charter. When Bede's *Ecclesiastical History of the English People* replaced oral traditions, the English nation was beginning to enjoy the *benefit of clergy*—the fruits of literacy. The pages that follow provide the background for the detailed discussion of the rise of Anglo-Saxon literacy that occupies Chapters 1 and 2.

2

THE COUNTRY AND ITS PEOPLES

A description of early Anglo-Saxon England cannot begin better than with that which Bede, England's first historian, offered in the introduction to his work. Bede starts by localizing Britain within a Roman imperial perspective—north and west of Europe—and moves quickly to a consideration of the land's chief virtues:

> Britain is an island in the ocean. . . . It runs northward for 800 miles, and is 200 miles broad. . . . The island is rich in crops and trees of various kinds, and it is suited for grazing sheep and cattle, and vineyards are grown in some places. This land also produces birds of various kinds and marine animals, and [it abounds] in springs and waters full of fish. Seals, whales, and porpoises are often caught here, and various kinds of shell-fish and mussels are commonly taken. . . . The land also has salt-pits and hot water, and hot baths in various localities, suitable for every age and both sexes; it produces ores of copper and iron, lead and silver in masses. . . . As this island lies close under the very north of the world and the nights here are light in summer—so that often at midnight a question arises among the spectators, whether it is the evening gloaming or morning dawn.[1]

He is clearly not describing all of England; there is no mention of the rugged, nearly uninhabitable highlands that were already in his time the homelands of Celts—modern Celtic Cornwall, Scotland, and Wales. Probably because he did not himself travel, he fails to mention the rivers (see Figure 1.1, page 19) that make most of lowland England easily accessible or the system of Roman roads that crisscrosses the interior. Nor does he mention the dangerous, dense forests of the distant (from him) southeast—a major deterrent to travel there. By discussing the land in terms of its ability to sustain the inhabitants and their main industries, Bede offers a glimpse into their daily life and work. The land is good and livable— harsh only by comparison with that magical realm, Ireland:

[1] Thomas Miller, ed. and trans., *The Old English Version of Bede's Ecclesiastical History of the English People* (London: Oxford University Press, 1891), pp. 25–27.

Introduction

> Ireland . . . is far superior to Britain in the breadth of its conformation and in salubrity and mildness of climate, so that snow seldom lies there for more than three days. No one there mows hay or builds stalls for his cattle, as a provision against winter's cold. No poisonous reptile is to be seen there, nor indeed may any viper live there; for vipers have been brought on board ship from Britain, but they died as soon as they smelt the air of the land.[2]

Within this setting of agricultural tranquility, Bede relates the bloody history of the violent invasion of the Germanic tribes and their conquest of the British:

> At that time [A.D. 449] the Angles and Saxons were called in. . . . They received settlements on the east side of the island by order of the same king who had invited them there to fight as for their country. They at once took the field against the foe, . . . and the Saxons won the victory. Then they sent home messengers, whom they bade to report the fertility of this land, and the cowardice of the Britons. . . . Then without delay they came in crowds. . . . And the people, who came here, began to increase and multiply to such an extent, that they were a great terror to the inhabitants themselves, who originally invited and called them in.[3]

The Angles settled northern and central England: Bede's forefathers took their name from their location north of the Humber River (Northumbrians); in the central regions, those who settled the west, near the western Celts, were known as the *Mierce,* "boundary folk " (Mercians), and those who settled the eastern half as the East Anglians. The south third of England became the homeland of the West, South, and East Saxons, except for the extreme south-eastern territory of Kent. The bulk of the history is concerned with the bitter intertribal warfare, of which the following is typical:

> Penda, king of Mercia, led his host into the land of Northumbria, wasting and despoiling it far and wide with cruel carnage. At last he came to the royal city, named Bamborough; and seeing that the town

[2] Ibid., pp. 29–31.
[3] Ibid., pp. 51–53.

4

was so strong, that he could not by assault or investment destroy or capture it, he determined to burn it down.[4]

In his descriptive method, Bede draws a sharp contrast between the everyday life of workers and the lives of those who shaped Anglo-Saxon history. If we include Bede's own account of his monastic existence, we have the groups into which the West Saxon king, Alfred the Great (A.D. 871–899), divided his subjects—"those who pray, soldiers and workmen:"

> I was born on land, which is private property of this monastery. When I was seven years old, by the care of my kindred I was given over to be brought up and trained by the venerable abbot Benedict and afterwards by Ceolfrith. And I spent the whole time of my life afterwards in the precincts of the monastery; and I gave all zeal to study and meditate on Holy Scripture. And while observing regular discipline, with the daily charge of singing in church, it was ever sweet and delightful to me to study, teach or write.[5]

Social class among the soldiers and workmen was highly stratified and hierarchical. From the early codes of law, we learn of the following ranks:

ealdormon	the highest ranking local official, one of the king's retainers
gesith and *thegn*	landowning nobles
geneat	a free peasant who worked for and defended his lord
gebur	(which combined with *neah*, "near," yielded *neahgebor* from which we get *neighbor*), free-men who paid high rents in labor and produce
theow	a slave

The *ceorls* (*geneats* and *geburs*) formed the bulk of Anglo-Saxon society. The nation's farmers and tradesmen, the *ceorls*, shared most rights and obligations with their betters, the *thegns:*

---

[4] Ibid., pp. 201–203.
[5] Ibid., pp. 481–483.

They were liable to taxation and church dues, could be called upon for military service, and had the duty of attendance at legal assemblies. In return they had privileges, of owning land, of freedom to move from one part of the country to another, and a fixed measure of protection from the law.[6]

Hence the differences were largely in terms of wealth. A further difference, however, was that the *gesiths* and *thegns* were the companions (*comites* in the language of the charters) of kings. We know much more about their lives that we do of the lives of *ceorls* because of the special relationship between Germanic kings (more realistically they would be termed tribal chieftains) and their *comites*:

> Everywhere in the Germanic world the ruler, whether king or chief, was attended by a body-guard of well-born companions. No Germanic institution has a longer history. . . . Much that is characteristic of the oldest Germanic literature turns on the relationship between the companions and their lord. The sanctity of the bond between lord and man, the duty of defending and avenging a lord, the disgrace of surviving him, gave rise to situations in which English listeners were always interested. . . . There is no doubt that this literature represented real life. It was the personal reputation of a king which attracted retainers to his court, and it was a king's military household around which all early fighting centered.[7]

To be a lordless *thegn* was to be without a regular place in society— an outcast deprived of all of life's benefits (see the poetic selection quoted in the dedication of this book).

These social distinctions were so important that they were among the first things codified in the earliest Anglo-Saxon laws. The laws set a fixed price, *wergild*, "man-tax," which had to be paid if the man were killed. The *Law of the Mercians* valued a king at 7200 shillings, a *gesith* at 1200 shillings, a *ceorl* at 200 shillings. For

---

[6] R. I. Page, *Life in Anglo-Saxon England* (London: B. T. Batsford, 1970), p. 53.

[7] Frank Stenton, *Anglo-Saxon England* (Oxford: Oxford University Press, 1971), p. 302.

6

comparison, 120 shillings was the value of the standard unit of land, enough to sustain a family unit.

Bede again provides insight into the relationships between the social classes of workers and fighters in reporting the experience of one Imma, a young retainer of Ælfwine, king of Northumbria, in a battle against Æthelred of Mercia. Ælfwine's army was defeated, and Imma was left among the dead. After a day among the corpses, he recovered and began searching for his friends:

> While doing this he was met and seized by men from the enemy's army; and they brought him to their lord, who was a gesith of king Æthelred. When he asked him what he was, he feared to acknowledge that he was a follower of the king, so he declared that he was a man of the people, poor and married; and that he had joined the expedition in order to fetch supplies and food to the king's followers and their companions . . . those who looked at him more narrowly, perceived from his face and bearing and his words also, that he was not of the poorer class, as he said, but of noble descent.[8]

It was apparently a common occurrence for peasants to join military expeditions as support personnel. Even more enlightening is Bede's observation of the socially diagnostic speech habits which helped define one's place in society.

Young retainers like Imma banded together in *comitatus* groups of about a dozen. Such groups made up the core of a king's army. It is clear that Anglo-Saxon social structure at its upper end was based on the roles of warriors. In fact, early kingship meant little more than fortuitous success at military leadership. Kings were made, not born; authority often did not extend beyond a tribe of a hundred or so families. Kings supported their households by taxing the land which they helped their supporters defend. From a charter of Offa, we learn what that tax, Old English *feorm*—the source of Modern English *farm*—amounted to for an estate which might support 60 families: "Two tuns full of pure ale and a coomb full of mild ale and a comb full of Welsh ale, and seven oxen and

---

[8] Miller, *Bede's History*, pp. 327–329.

six wethers and 40 cheeses and six long *peru* and 30 ambers of unground corn and four ambers of meal."[9] Most of these measures are obscure, but if taken in proportion to the oxen and cheeses, we can be sure that a king's household ate and drank well enough to justify the reports of feasting and beer drinking in the heroic poetry.

The sort of rigor involved in establishing a man's value was essential given the violent nature of life in early Anglo-Saxon England. Not only were kings and subkings constantly at war, but the warfare was savage. The *Anglo-Saxon Chronicle* regularly records mutilation, blinding, scalping, and the taking of slaves. Good St. Guthlac, a Mercian prince, gained his reputation by burning and plundering the villages and manors of his enemies. It is a measure of his piety that he returned a third of his plunder to its owners—an eighth century version of Robin Hood. Even without war, life was harsh; plague and famine were commonplace in the annals of the *Chronicle*. Excavations of early cemeteries suggest high infant mortality rates and a general life expectancy of about 35. Even within this grim context, everyday life had its benefits. The descriptions of representative individuals from *The Endowments of Men* ought to temper our views of those times:

> To one he granteth possessions here on earth,
> worldly treasures. One is hapless,
> a luckless wight, yet is he skilled
> in crafts of the mind. One receiveth in greater measure
> bodily strength. One is comely,
> beauteous of form. One is a poet,
> gifted with song. One is eloquent.
> One goeth a-hunting, a pursuer
> of ferocious beasts. One is dear
> to the man of worldly power. One is stout-hearted in battle,
> a martial hero, when the shields clash.
> One in the council of sagacious men
> may deliberate on a nation's law,

[9] Dorothy Whitelock, *English Historical Documents c. 500–1042* (London: Eyre and Spottiswoode, 1955), p. 467.

where many sages meet together . . .
One with his hands can greet the harp:
he hath skill in the glee-beam's prompt pulsations.
One is a runner; one a sure archer . . .
One is pious, diligent in alms,
virtuously good. One is a well-known thane
in the mead-hall. One is skilled in managing the steed,
wise in all horse-craft. One, self-controlled,
suffereth in patience whatsoever he must.
One understands the laws, when people
seek counsel. One is expert at dice.
One is witty at wine-bibbing,
a good beer-keeper.[10]

Bede reminds us that the pleasures of the mead-hall and general domestic peace were possible when a king was strong enough:

It is said, that in those times there was such peace in Britain, everywhere around where Eadwine had authority, though a woman should go alone with her new-born child, she might proceed without injury from sea to sea all over this island.[11]

Germanic tribal society, with a heroic ethic as its base, survived the transplantation to Britain with little, if any, change. It could not, however, remain unchanged with the introduction of Christianity.

THE CONVERSION

Although there had been Christians in England during the Roman period, the Germanic conquest of Britain was a temporary triumph for paganism. Christianity reentered England from two directions. In A.D. 597, the Roman mission sent St. Augustine into the southeastern kingdom of Kent. In A.D. 565, Columba, an Irish Celt of

---

[10] Israel Gollancz, *The Exeter Book* (London: Oxford University Press, 1895), pp. 295–297.

[11] Miller, *Bede's History*, p. 145.

royal blood, had established a monastery at Iona; from there, Celtic Christianity with its emphasis on monasticism diffused into Northumbria. The Celtic influence was not so much a separate variety of Christianity as a version of Roman Christianity filtered through Celtic Ireland:

> In all essentials of organization and doctrine the expanding Church remained thoroughly Roman. As the fourth century evidence shows, the British Church, like the Church everywhere else in the Empire, modelled its organization on that of the civil government; its bishops were established in the principal towns, which were centres both of civic and religious administration. . . . Yet the highland zone of Britain had few towns and during these years of expansion Britain was falling back into a congeries of tribal kingdoms. In this area and in Ireland diocesan organization was retained, but adapted to conform to the requirements of tribal kingdoms.[12]

St. Patrick himself emphasized his position as bishop and clearly thought he had founded a church governed by bishops.

Gregory's plans for England were explicitly diocesan. He intended there to be two archbishoprics, each governing 12 bishops. Because of his master plan, the southern church developed a strong administrative structure which it could use to support the emerging kingdoms of the next centuries and, by the way, insure that Roman Christianity would be the dominant form in England. It is well to remember, however, that the contrast between the two approaches to Christianity was merely one of focus and style. The Celts specialized in the contemplative life and its fruits; the Romans made virtues of organization and discipline.

The actual conversion of the Germanic tribes was a slow process with much backsliding. It was necessary to begin by converting kings, whose subjects usually followed suit, if unwillingly. At first, the kings unfortunately were more often moved by utility than by piety. Given the violent tenor of the times, even the most earnest conversion of a king could not be counted on as a long-range affair.

[12] D. J. V. Fisher, *The Anglo-Saxon Age* (London: Longman, 1973), pp. 58–59.

By small steps and with great good luck, Christianity not only became the religion of England, it became the official religion. The church's first, and immediate, success with King Æthelberht of Kent made possible a missionary effort in Northumbria. The result was the conversion of kings like Edwin who were lavish in their support. Because of this close association with Northumbrian kings, the episcopal structure of the English church was strengthened and became an administrative outlet for fervor generated by Celtic monasticism. The Roman church received a rich endowment—one of the most sophisticated literate communities in the medieval world.

As soon as the church was well established in Britain, the newly converted Germanic tribes looked with missionary zeal back at the still pagan homeland. During the age of Bede, scores of monasteries and bishoprics were founded in Germanic Europe. That missionary activity is the strongest testament to the health and power of the English church; an effort of such magnitude was certainly expensive. In the process of organizing the church so that it could bear the expense, Theodore, archbishop of Canterbury, made an innovation that would later make possible the organization of the political kingdoms. He drafted written records, modeled on the private charters of the later Roman Empire, by which kings confirmed their gifts to the church. As in the case of the later charters of the Mercian kings, "these charters were meant to surround and protect grants of privilege with the awful majesty of the written word."[13] Writing became an integral part of the establishment of the power structures in Anglo-Saxon England. A strong church required the security that strong governments can provide.

THE KING AND HIS ALTAR-THANES

Roman diocesan organization was patterned after imperial structures. It was natural for both early bishops and kings to sense the

[13] Eric John, *Orbis Britanniae* (Leicester: Leicester University Press, 1966), p. 3.

mutual benefit to be derived from cooperation. As archbishops ruled bishops who ruled clergy, they could expect to be received as the peers of the king's closest counselors. As members of royal families took holy orders and often themselves founded monasteries, the connection between a secular and religious aristocracy became fixed. In this era, kings regularly abdicated in order to live out their last days in monastic contemplation. In such a cultural climate, the *Laws of Æþelred* contain no surprise when they proclaim a priest to be a *weofodthegn*, "altar-thane," with the same *wergild* as the king's own thanes. Just as clearly, the religion which named Christ "King of Kings," with its tradition of just kings ruling as God's chosen, could dignify the position of tribal warlords aspiring to kingship.

Notions of Germanic kingship underwent complete revision in the Anglo-Saxon period under the influence of the cultural residue of Christian imperial Rome. The early Anglo-Saxon kings imitated the Roman legal system and experimented in writing laws self-consciously echoing Latin formulae. With the further support from the church, they could come to view themselves as the vessels of God's own justice. It is not likely accidental that the first laws were decrees of the first convert, King Æþelberht, and are thus contemporary with Augustine's mission. If kings are lawmakers, then surely the bishops are his appropriate advisors. Æþelberht's laws explicitly protect the properties of the church; soon laws would deal with such religious matters as marriage and Sunday observance. With a literate clergy at hand, the functions of the king could turn from exclusive concern with warfare. A king could demonstrate, and give permanent substance to, his power by writing laws, drafting royal decrees, and issuing charters, as well as by defeating all foes. With rudimentary administrative organization would come more efficient taxation. Soon Anglo-Saxon kings would again follow imperial example and issue their own coins.

None of this is to suggest that administrative efficiency was Christianity's main attraction to the early Anglo-Saxon monarchs. Many of them, as no less than St. Bede himself assures us, were men of genuine piety. Of all of Bede's beautiful prose, his most striking metaphor is the one by which he describes the power of the argument which resulted in the conversion of Edwin:

> "O king, the present life of man on earth, in comparison with the time unknown to us, seems to me, as if you sat at table with your chief men and followers in winter time, and a fire was kindled and your hall warmed, while it rained, snowed, and stormed without; and there came a sparrow and swiftly flew through the house, entering at one door and passing out through the other. Now as long as he is inside, he is not pelted with winter's storm; but that is the twinkling of an eye and a moment of time, and at once he passes back from winter into winter. So then this life of man appears for but a little while; what goes before, or what comes after, we know not. So if this new doctrine reports anything more certain or apt, it deserves to be followed."[14]

It is an accident of our history that that doctrine was preserved by a literate tradition, and that literacy would be the means of strengthening the power of kings and widening the potential sphere of their protection.

[14] Miller, *Bede's History*, pp. 135–137.

I

LITERACY AND POLITICS IN EARLY ANGLO-SAXON ENGLAND

NGLO-SAXONISTS assume that the early English built primarily with wood and left behind for our study no enduring monuments of stonework such as the Romans left as a record of their involvement in early British history. Similarly, others would point out that we who are cultural descendants of the early English seem to have little in our social, cultural, and temperamental make-up that we owe directly to our Germanic forebears. Thus, even though we speak a language that is a lineal (though bastard) descendant of Old English, that language has changed—just as dramatically as have the nature and needs of its speakers.

All of these statements are true enough; they are less a testimony to historical myopia than an acknowledgment of historical fact. They ignore a real, if less obvious, accomplishment of the early Anglo-Saxon period: learning to write the English language. A nearly universal, vernacular literacy so pervades our lives, our culture, our social and political structures that we speakers of English can take it for granted. Surely, the idea of vernacular literacy did not originate in England, but the impulse of our forebears to experiment with writing their own speech greatly affected the development and dissemination of Western European modes of thought. Like Bede and Alcuin, we too love learning and write our intellectual histories. Unlike them, but because of them and their time, we need not write our histories in another's language. We pay unconscious tribute to them as we conduct the business of literacy in our mother tongue, which they knew only how to speak. Bede's Latin history, replete as it is with Old English names for Roman and Celtic places, attests our early inclination to "have our own word for it." The greatest

Latin scholar of his time, Bede also pioneered the translation into English of important texts, though unfortunately none of them survives, and he urged that the clergy be able to teach the rudiments of Christian doctrine in English. The principle was so important to him that he spent his waning energies in the act of dictating from his deathbed a translation of St. John's Gospel. His students felt it worth reporting that St. Bede chose to sing his death song in our English speech.

It was, then, during the time of Bede that we first tried to write the language of our speech. Customs and traditions are transitory and easily mutable until they become written; the work of such contemporary anthropologists as Jack Goody documents the profound effects of the development of writing on human societies. Certainly as modern speakers and/or writers of Standard English, we know perhaps more than we care to about the use of literacy in the establishment and maintenance of power structures. When as speakers of Old English we learned to write our speech, we learned to build our most permanent monuments. It is our Anglo-Saxon heritage that we chose as material neither wood nor stone—but the ink and parchment of the written word.

It is a happy coincidence for historical linguists that the first attempts to write English contain evidence for the study of language change. The scribes who left us the record did not intend to be writing linguistic history; they were conducting their varied businesses—writing charters, glossing texts, compiling glossaries, etc. The present work assumes that any study based on a written tradition must first be a study of literacy, its uses, and its effects. Before we can use the data of the oldest English texts to reconstitute the speech of the scribes who wrote them, we are obliged to know as well as possible the contexts that impelled those acts of literacy. Consequently, the first concern of this study will be to offer a historical sketch of the political, social, and economic situation in which Anglo-Saxons first experimented in writing English. This first chapter argues that the disparate Anglo-Saxon tribes began to be (and to think of themselves as) an English nation just when they began to be writers of our English language.

1 Literacy and Politics in Early Anglo-Saxon England

Although no fully explicit contemporary accounts survive, Anglo-Saxonists are able to piece together a coherent description of the process by which the Germanic invaders of post-Roman Britain became an English nation. Details are few and only fortuitously attested; although they are sufficient to provide a clear outline of received facts, they are not so extensive as to preclude speculation and scholarly debate. All agree that the early settlement/conquest of Britain was essentially a piecemeal, tribal affair. By A.D. 600, the larger, more powerful tribes had consolidated themselves into the seven kingdoms of the so-called Anglo-Saxon Heptarchy—Northumbria, Mercia, East Anglia, Wessex, Essex, Sussex, and Kent (see Figure 1.1). The kings were locally powerful warlords who managed temporarily to secure a tenuous influence over their eventual usurpers. Few died of old age; fewer still passed their title on to an immediate heir. According to Bede, an overlord was occasionally able to gain hegemony over neighboring kingdoms. Even though the traditional view of early Anglo-Saxon political structure emphasized hegemony almost to the point of misrepresentation, it is a useful first approximation. Three kingdoms, each with successively greater influence, were able to extend their domination beyond their native realms: the Northumbrians (c. A.D. 625–675), the Mercians (c. A.D. 650–825), and the West Saxons (c. A.D. 800–1050). These were periods of relative stability but not absolute continuity in succession of authority.

LITERACY IN THE EARLY ANGLO-SAXON KINGDOMS

Of particular interest is the fact that in each of the three cases some degree of political stability occasioned a flowering of learning. The Northumbrian kings, for example, established the monasteries of Wearmouth and Jarrow—which ultimately produced Bede and Alcuin, the famous school at York, and the finest library in Europe. So great was the achievement that Charlemagne looked to the

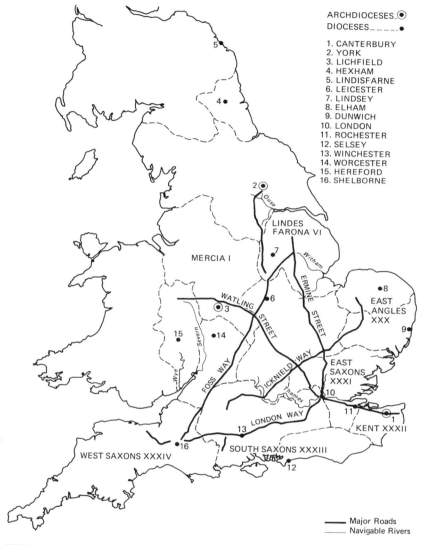

LINDES
FARONA VI

MERCIA I

WATLING STREET

ERMINE STREET

EAST
ANGLES
XXX

FOSS WAY

ICKNIELD WAY

EAST
SAXONS
XXXI

LONDON WAY

KENT XXXII

WEST SAXONS XXXIV

SOUTH SAXONS XXXIII

— Major Roads
— Navigable Rivers

FIGURE 1.1. Early Anglo-Saxon England. (Roman numerals refer to locations of major tribal groups listed in *Tribal Hidage*.)

1 Literacy and Politics in Early Anglo-Saxon England

Northumbrian wealth of learning, inviting Alcuin to establish a school in his court. Indeed, the Bible as we know it owes much to Wearmouth and Jarrow. The most authoritative version of the Latin Vulgate text is preserved in the *Codex Amiatinus*. It was one of three complete Bibles produced around A.D. 715 in Northumbria— each over 1000 leaves of quality vellum (27.5 inches by 20.5 inches, or 70 cm by 50 cm), weighing in excess of 75 pounds (35 kg). The immense cost of such a production is a poignant measure of Anglo-Saxon dedication to the Word and hence a direct indication of the importance of literacy to Anglo-Saxon kings. King Ceolwulf, we also know, paid personal attention to the production of Bede's *Ecclesiastical History;* he read and criticized a draft of it. We ought to be less than surprised to see Bede pay full tribute to the power of Northumbrian kings as rulers of all England, while politicly ignoring in that passage the competing, supreme Mercian ruler of southern England. King Ceolwulf and Bede knew the power of the written word. They would not be surprised to learn that modern histories have perpetuated a picture which political fact did not justify, in that contemporary scholars have uncritically accepted Bede's northern perspective. Later Anglo-Saxon kings read their Bede and learned their lesson: An educated clergy can be more than a mere luxurious adornment to a dignified court.

Hegemony was developed into something more like genuine kingship during the West Saxon period; William conquered England in the act of subduing one English king. The period also produced a wealth of written products in the language of the people and their king. Because almost all of the surviving Old English texts date from the West Saxon period, and because they are written in a very regular, standardized literary language, the West Saxon dialect is often equated with Old English. Even those who avoid this oversimplification continue to expect of earlier texts the linguistic homogeneity of the West Saxon productions. Further, it must be remembered that West Saxon texts reflect a southwestern view of reality just as certainly as Bede's history reflects a Northumbrian perspective. The only extant chronicle from the period is the West Saxon version of the *Anglo-Saxon Chronicle*. Its writers chose for

20

perfectly understandable reasons to join Bede in ignoring the extent of Mercian domination. They were in fact using Bede as a major source of information and may simply have incorporated his view. More probably, they were providing an account of early history for the satisfaction and use of West Saxon kings. The West Saxons were the immediate conquerors of the Mercians; the exigencies of hegemony would not encourage a faithful assertion of Mercian strength.

The Mercian hegemony bridges the gap between Northumbria's first attempts at the political unification of what is now England and the West Saxon accomplishment of that fact. Clearly the Mercian period was one of continuing consolidation of power; it was also the period that produced the first texts written in English. Unfortunately, it failed to produce either its own local historian of Bede's stature or a surviving independent chronicle tradition, such as that which facilitates the reconstruction of West Saxon history. That is, the texts that survive, though they are fairly extensive, form a forbidding mass of secondary sources which needs to be gleaned painstakingly for fragments of evidence. As a result, the Mercian period has been understudied, and the contributions of the Mercians to the development of English political and literate culture have been undervalued.[1] One consequence of an easier West Saxon perspective for Old English studies has been to overemphasize the role that Alfred the Great (A.D. 871–899) played in the development of English letters. The position of a teacher–king as a force in the establishment of a standard written variety can not be underestimated, but he functioned as a reviver and extender of literate traditions rather than as their sole originator. The comment with which he begins his translation of the *Pastoral Care* is that of a reformer. He was probably overstating the decay of learning in England. More importantly, while he complains about the decay of Latin literacy, he affirms, "yet many could read English writing."[2] The current

[1] R. Vleeskruyer, ed., *The Life of St. Chad* (Amsterdam: North-Holland Publishing Company, 1953), pp. 39–42.

[2] Henry Sweet, ed., *King Alfred's West-Saxon Version of Gregory's Pastoral Care* (Oxford: Oxford University Press, 1871), p. 3.

level of native literacy could only have been a Mercian achievement. We have further evidence that Alfred drew on a strong base of Mercian scholarship in his efforts to further extend vernacular literacy. Four of his seven chief aides in that task were learned Mercians. The difficulties of reconstructing, from such data as can be assembled, the nature and context of that Mercian cultural achievement are not insurmountable. The reward of understanding the situation in which we began to be a literate nation justifies the expense of effort. Because the narrative that follows is based on a reappraisal of original manuscript data and a fresh piecing together of bits of historical evidence in the light of contemporary methods, it is almost necessarily revisionist.

Early Political Structure

The *Tribal Hidage* is one of our most important single resources for understanding the political and social structure of early Anglo-Saxon England. The text survives in several early manuscripts—one Old English manuscript of the eleventh century (*British Museum Harley 3271,* 6v) and six later Latin texts. The document is a list of the names of tribal groups (generally found in the possessive plural), each of which is assigned a numerical assessment in hides. The text is important enough to reproduce fully in its Old English version in which Roman numerals refer to locations on Figure 1.1 and major groups are identified by their modern English names:

    I. Myrcna landes 30,000—the Mercians
    II. Wocen sætna 7000—the Wrekin-dwellers
  III. Westerna 7000—the Westerners
  IV. Pecsætna 1200
    V. Elmed sætna 600
  VI. Lindesfarona 7000—Lindsey and Hatfield Chase
 VII. Suþ gyrwa 600
      Norþ gyrwa 600

VIII. East wixna 300
 West wixna 300
 IX. Spalda 600
 X. Wigesta 900
 XI. Herefinna 1200
 XII. Sweord ora 300
 XIII. Gifla 300
 XIV. Hicca 300
 XV. Wiht gara 600
 XVI. Nox gaga 5000—??
 Oht gaga 2000
 XVII. Hwinca 7000—the Hwicce
 XVIII. Ciltern sætna 4000—the Chilterns
 XIX. Hendrica 3500—Berkshire
 XX. Unecung ga 1200
 XXI. Aro sætna 600
 XXII. Færpinga 300
 XXIII. Bilmiga 600
 XXIV. Widerigga 600
 XXV. East willa 600
 West willa 600
 XXVI. East engle 30,000—the East Angles
 XXVII. East sexena 7000—the East Saxons
 XXVIII. Cant warena 15,000—the Kentish
 XXIX. Suþ sexena 7000—the South Saxons
 XXX. West sexena 100,000—the West Saxons

As the term *hide* originally designated a nuclear family or the land needed to support a nuclear family (fixed in the later medieval period at 120 acres), it is clear that this document is some sort of census list. No one has ever doubted that the list was drawn up from a Mercian perspective. First, none of the folk north of the Humber River are included. Further the opening entry, *Myrcna landes is þrittig þusend hyda þaer mon aerest myrcna haet*, "the Mercians' land, that is, of those first called Mercians," establishes the focus of the list while implying that the current influence of the Mercians has spread. "No one in the seventh or eighth century can be imagined compiling such a document out of mere curiosity. It only becomes intelligible when it is regarded as an attempt to guide a king's ministers in the exaction of his dues from subject provinces."[3] That king was no doubt an early Mercian overlord, and internal evidence points to Wulfhere (A.D. 657–674) or Æþelred (A.D. 674–704),[4] although as late as Offa is a possibility.[5] Clearly, the stability of these early kingdoms and the ability to levy tribute were tightly interwoven.

It is notable that the census is organized not according to strict geographical divisions but tribally; territory is viewed in terms of inhabitants rather than boundaries. Importantly, three major classifications of peoples emerge: the very large—the kingdoms of the Mercians (30,000), the East Anglians (30,000), the Kentish (15,000), the West Saxons (100,000); the medium sized—the Hwicca (7000), the Lindesfarona (7000), the Chilterns (4000), etc.; the small (often as yet unlocalized)—in multiples of 300. The largest are easily identified as the major tribal groups that vied for control of southern England during this period, groups whose kings were powerful enough to grant land and privilege in their own right. The middle groups were still substantial, but dependent. Their leaders might call themselves king, but they are known to us from documents in which they are designated as *ministers* to or *subreguli* of their Mercian overlords. The leaders of the smallest tribes constitute the *comites*, the *principes*, the *duces*, and the ealdormen of the major documents. An administrative hierarchy is clear. One of the major kingdoms (in this case the Mercians) would be in control, with the middle groups subject directly to them. "By contrast, the Tribal

[3] F. M. Stenton, *Anglo-Saxon England*, 3rd ed. (Oxford: Oxford University Press, 1971), p. 297.

[4] Wendy Davies and Hayo Vierck, "The Contexts of Tribal Hidage: Social Aggregates and Settlement Patterns," *Frühmittelalterliche Studien* 8 (1974): p. 227.

[5] Cyril Hart, "The Tribal Hidage," *Transactions of the Royal Historical Society*, 5th series, 21 (1971): pp. 133–157.

Hidage small groups form *no* part of a larger unit; between them and their Mercian overlord there is no larger negotiation power."[6] The power of one kingdom might extend over its peer kingdoms for a time, but the basic fabric of Anglo-Saxon society during the Mercian period was still tribal in nature. Political unification would depend upon an overlord's ability to effect a confederation of large and small tribal groups. Tribal organization obviates strict territorial division of the south of England into just Mercia, Wessex, East Anglia, Essex, Sussex, and Kent, as the smaller groups clearly played an important role in an overlord's economic (hence political) base. Further, it calls into question two standard assumptions of English historical linguistics: first, the geographical orientation of the dialectology proposed for early English, with its oversimplified division of the country into Northumbrian, Mercian, West Saxon, and Kentish; and, second, the further assumption that each of the four regional varieties was a single, homogeneous speech variety. Tribal organization is not a likely foundation for widespread linguistic homogeneity.

LITERACY AND THE ESTABLISHMENT OF MERCIAN POLITICAL ASCENDANCY

The Mercian kings rose from the obscurity of preliterate times when they were first converted to Christianity (and thus had recourse to the benefits of a literate clergy). Penda (A.D. 632–655) was the first of the strongest (and the last of the pagan) Mercian overlords, but we would know little beyond his name had he not attracted Bede's attention as among Northumbria's most formidable enemies. Although it is unclear whether the other kings of the south were strictly subject to him, he was certainly foremost among them and their leader in the battles against Northumbria. By virtue of defeating Penda, Oswiu of Northumbria could claim the title of overlord of the Mercians and the rest of the southern English.

[6] Davies and Vierck, "Tribal Hidage," p. 240.

1 Literacy and Politics in Early Anglo-Saxon England

Penda's son Wulfhere (A.D. 657–674) was able, after a brief reversal of Mercian fortunes, to reconsolidate and then extend his father's influence. After conquering the West Saxons, he demonstrated that he was supreme by making a grant of traditionally West Saxon territory to Æþelwalh, the king of the South Saxons. The unusual occasion at which the grant was made is recorded by Bede:

> Æþelwalh, king of that people, shortly before had received baptism in Mercia, owing to the prompting and the zeal of the Mercian king Wulfhere . . . he took him as god-son, and in token of amity made over to him two provinces.[7]

Wulfhere is not simply using his authority to help spread the faith; he also is just as clearly using his position as the guardian of the faith to demonstrate the extent of his political control. In the same act, he is taking land (power base) away from a strong rival and using it to create a friendly dependent. This Mercian warlord added new dimensions to his secular authority as he began to act regularly in a fashion befitting a Christian king: He gave land (in Lindsey, a previously Northumbrian province) to Chad for the founding of a monastery; he sold the episcopal see of London to a bishop who had recently been expelled from Wessex by Wulfhere's enemy King Cenwahl; he sent his own bishop to Essex to quell a reversion to paganism. To notice that these acts enhanced Wulfhere's political position is not to question his piety, but rather to emphasize the interdependence of the development of early Mercian concepts of kingship and the involvement of the kings in the affairs of the church.

The coalition was genuinely synergistic in that it produced written documentation of its effects. Kings could grant land and privileges; religious could record and witness the act. Working cooperatively, both parties could produce a written document, a charter which

[7] Thomas Miller, ed., *The Old English Version of Bede's Ecclesiastical History of the English People, Part I, 2* (1891; rpt. Oxford: Oxford University Press, 1959), p. 303.

manifested elements of authority which neither party could effect independently. Overlords and their scribes might make charters, but charters made kings and kingship official. They constituted, in the substance of written words, concrete and permanent evidence of political structure. One might argue whether "the pen is mightier than the sword," but their combined might is not arguable. We have already seen evidence of Wulfhere's expanding authority and might wonder, along with his contemporaries, if he deserves a title which better describes the expanding role of Mercian kings. We recognize a new element in Mercian hegemony when we find a charter recording a land grant by King Friþuwold of Surrey, "subking of Wulfhere," confirmed by Wulfhere and witnessed by four other subkings. The charter gave substance to the kingly state.

It is noteworthy that the reign of the second of Penda's sons, Æðelred (A.D. 674–704), is more important for the history of the English church than for the Mercian hegemony. Famous for the generosity with which he granted land to the church throughout his realm, Æðelred confirmed the close working relationship between the kings of Mercia and the church. A king who could claim he was *Christo largiente rex,* "king through the grace of Christ," was no mere barbarian warlord to be challenged at whim.

Precisely because they are more than a simple record of a king's activities, the early charters are the major source of information about the process by which the Mercian kings made a political institution out of a military hegemony. The charters reflect an evolution of royal prerogative and provide evidence of the ever more complex administrative structures needed to execute that prerogative. The titles of respect that individual kings employed record the terms in which the kings viewed themselves, stated their kingship, and defined their relationships to their client subkings. Placenames within the charters attest the geographical extent of a king's influence and inform us where he regularly held court. The names in the witness lists give an indication of the extent of a king's reputation among the secular and religious nobles of his time. Such conclusions must have been just as evident to the makers and readers of Anglo-Saxon

27

charters. It is not likely mere coincidence that royal authority increased concomitantly with the development of resources enabling the official documentation of authority.

The King of the English People

The full potential of Wulfhere's experiment in institutionalizing political control was realized during the reigns of Æþelbald (A.D. 716–757) and Offa the Great (A.D. 757–796). This 80-year period of relative political unification and stability was a remarkable first in early Anglo-Saxon history. Even Bede, who elsewhere had been able to ignore the Mercian dynasty, ended his history with a political survey of A.D. 731, in which he was forced to recognize the extent of the rising influence of Mercia:

> And all these provinces and also other southern provinces, so far as the boundary of the river Humber, with their kings also, are subject in obedience to Æþelbald, king of Mercia.[8]

The charters that survive from this period record a self-conscious attempt to make formal, to document, the unambiguous control that the Mercian kings exercised over submissive local subkings.

A charter of A.D. 736 confirms Bede's statement and describes Æðelbald as "king not only of the Mercians but also of all the provinces which are called by the general name 'South English.'" The witness list makes the assertion even more boldly: *Aethelbald rex Britanniae*, "Æðelbald, king of Britain." The local King Æðelric of the Hwicce, within whose territory this grant of land was made, is rendered "underking and companion of the most glorious prince Æðelbald."[9] The documents from his reign record Æðelbald's widespread involvement in the affairs of Berkshire, Gloucestershire, Herefordshire, Middlesex, Warwickshire, Wiltshire, and Worces-

---

[8] Miller, *Bede Part I. 2*, p. 479.
[9] Dorothy Whitelock, *English Historical Documents, Volume I. c. 500–1042* (London: Eyre & Spottiswoode, 1955), pp. 453–454.

tershire. The Wiltshire Charter (conveying land within the boundaries of Wessex) was witnessed, but not authored, by King Cynewulf of Wessex and several West Saxon nobles and bishops. Æðelbald's control of London is clear from the fact that he regularly collected tolls from ships in the major city of *his* realm. That toll may well have been collected in the very coinage recently attributed to Æðelbald's reign.[10] (Offa had previously been held the only Mercian coiner of note.) The iconography of the coins is telling: The *cynehelm*, "crown-helmet" of the Anglo-Saxon warrior-kings, and the cross—the two major instruments of Æðelbald's successful ascendancy—figure prominently.

In A.D. 735, York became an independent archiepiscopal see, limiting the see of Canterbury to southern England (that is, Mercian England). Æðelbald took full advantage of the situation to institutionalize his position as *Bretwalda* by presiding jointly with the archbishop of Canterbury (*his* archbishop, after all) over assemblies of all of the leading secular and religious leaders of the south. At the Synod of Clovesho in A.D. 742, it was Æðelbald who confirmed the privileges of the church in Kent, privileges originally granted by Wihtred of Kent and now confirmed by the Mercian King of Britain. As king, Æðelbald was able to demand and get, even in the face of the strongest of opposition from St. Boniface, a levy of support on church land holdings for the repair of bridges and maintenance of fortifications. That, in addition to his infamous personal lifestyle, probably inspired St. Boniface's vision of Æðelbald in hell (in the unhappy company of a host of unbaptized West Saxon babies). Throughout his reign, Æðelbald was careful to maintain good relations with the church; he granted land for no fewer than five religious foundations and regularly remitted on the behalf of the church the toll on ships at his port of London. Even his strong critic St. Boniface was forced to credit him for his achievements, "you strongly prohibit theft and iniquities, perjury and rapine, and

---

[10] D. M. Metcalf, "Monetary Affairs in Mercia in the time of Æthelbald," in Ann Dornier, ed., *Mercian Studies* (Leicester: Leicester University Press, 1977), pp. 87–106.

. . . you are known to be a defender of widows and the poor, and . . . you maintain firm peace in your kingdom."[11] The fact that Æðelbald was murdered by his own bodyguard is poignant testimony to the violent tenor of life in even the most stable of Anglo-Saxon times.

Æðelbald's confederacy dissolved during a period of civil war in Mercia which followed his murder, but his distant cousin Offa was able to restore peace so quickly that the years of his reign nominally begin with the year of Æðelbald's death. Offa's ability to recoup and then to extend Æðelbald's authority reminds us how dependent the success of early kingship was upon the strong personality of kings, but certainly the security of hegemony also had its attractions: After having enjoyed the benefits of Æðelbald's long and peaceful reign, subkings must have seen the advantages of trading a title, vacuous in anarchy, for the protection of a strong overlord. The kings of the Hwicce acknowledged officially their status as underkings to Offa, *rex Merciorum*, within 2 years of Æðelbald's death (by A.D. 759). By A.D. 764, Offa had reestablished some measure of control in the southeast, as the following facts evidence: He confirmed Æþelbald's remission of toll at London for the minster at Thanet, with the king of Kent and the archbishop of Canterbury attesting; and, in the same year, he confirmed grants of land in Kent. The Kentish kings, in the next year, sent a grant of land at Rochester to Peterborough for Offa's confirmation. In A.D. 767, Iænberht, archbishop of Canterbury, and the bishops of Leicester and Lichfield were willing to witness Offa's grant of land in Middlesex. Osmund, the king of the South Saxons, witnessed one of Offa's charters (A.D. 772) as *dux*, simply "ealdorman."

Two dealings with subkings demonstrate clearly the expansion of Offa's powers. Not only was he granting lands throughout England at will, he was further able to annul one of Egbert of Kent's grants and confiscate the subject lands. A subking, he argued, could not give to another what was given him by his overlord except with his overlord's permission. A charter (A.D. 780) of Oslac, an ealdorman

[11] Whitelock, *English Historical Documents*, p. 752.

of Sussex, constitutes the first "direct evidence that an Anglo-Saxon king has writers in his employment whom he can use for official business. The charter itself if written in a crude and apparently unpractised hand . . . Offa's endorsement is written in a typical insular hand of the period."[12] (See Figure 1.2.) Offa's personal royal scriptorium marks the creation of a professional learned class whose express concern it was to record "the king's English."

It is at first surprising that a king of Offa's stature would choose as his most frequent title *rex Merciorum*, "king of the Mercians." It may well be that, after Æþelbald, *rex Merciorum* implied *rex Britanniae*, as Offa did occasionally have his title recorded in the fuller form, *rex Merciorum simulque aliarum circumquaque nationum*, "king of the Mercians and surrounding nations." After all, Egbert of Wessex, only 30 years after Offa's death, called himself *rex Merciorum*, apparently to express the fact that he was supreme in the south. Two Kentish grants to Archbishop Iænberht refer to Offa in the most extravagant terms that had ever been applied to an Anglo-Saxon king—*rex Anglorum*, "king of the English," and *rex totius Anglorum patriae*, "king of all England." Although these last two titles appear in tenth-century copies, Stenton accepted them as faithful to the language of their eighth-century originals: "The phrase is important as a contemporary gloss upon the most important of English regnal styles at the moment of its first appearance."[13]

At the same time he was using the charter formulae to assert his position as king, Offa subtly began to make changes in the substance of what charters did and did not grant or exempt. Earlier charters assumed future immunity from public burdens, such as food-rent, to the king, but such exemption was not, before Offa, made explicit. In the process of specifying freedom from "tribute," Offa made it *literally*, "by letters," clear that three obligations could never be lifted: fortress work, bridge work, and military duty. These

---

[12] F. M. Stenton, *The Latin Charters of the Anglo-Saxon Period* (Oxford: Oxford University Press, 1955), p. 37.

[13] Doris Mary Stenton, ed., *Preparatory to Anglo-Saxon England* (Oxford: Oxford University Press, 1970), p. 60, n. 6.

+ REX ANGL̄ Inperpetuum · Ihū nō ihu xp̄o ac ꝫuber
nance ꝙ egꝛ oꝛ ac duxturꝯ saxoꝛum aliquant terre
parte mp̄kꝓ ꝛe mediͦ ioanimi meae uenerabile ecclē
egꝛ ipauli poꝛ toti liberte concede id ꝛ duo nomini
ꝺur ꝑna ꝼ ach tiele ꝼ oꝛa umomnib; ꝼa de um p̄r tin
ꝼacͭ ume ꝼ th ioc oꝯ appellaͭ u ꝼ iolet ae iꞇ
+ Ego ꝼ la han donac ionem ꝓpꝛia manu ꝓsubscripꞇ ·
+ Ego ꝛ her e epͭ conſenͭ ſ ſubſcripſiꞇ + Ego eld dunſ ꝼ
conſenſiaꞇ ſ ſubſcripſi + Ego ✠ ...al conſenſ ſ ſubscripſiꞇ +
Ego u c̄mͭ oꞁ conſenſ ꞇ al ſcripſ ꞇ Ego oꞇ oꝛmoꝯ conſenꞇ ꞇ
ſ ſubscripſ ꞇ Ego uertꝛꝺ conſenſ ꞇ a conſenſ al ſcripſ ꞇ Egoꝛ al
obꞇ ian conſenͭ ꞇ ꞇ ꝼ ſcripꞇ ſ + Egoꝛ eff a conſenſ ꞇ ꞇ ſubſcripꞇ ꞇ + Egoꝛ al
+ Egoꝛ eald heaꝛd conſenꞇ ꞇ ꝼ ſubſcripſꞇ + Egoꝛ al ꝺ ꞇ ꝼ r̄ nuꝺ
conſenſ ꞇ a ꝼ ꝺ ſcripſꞇ + Egoꝛ ꝼoꝛm heaꝛd conſenꝼꞇ ꝼ ſubſcrop
l ꞇ ꞇ + Egoꝛ oͭ eoꝼꞇ nox conſenſ Eg ꞇ u ꝼcripſꞇ + Egoꝛe ꝫaluꝼ
omnꝼ ꝺ ꞇ ꞇ p̄ni ꝑꝺiciꞇ ꝼ ꞇ ꝼꝙ um ꞇ oꝛoc decꝛe tum IRRIT u m ꝼ́a
ꞇ ...ꝛ ꞇ ꞇ ꞇ ꝼ en... ad c ꞇ ꞇ ꞇ ꞇ k amme con a maꝓꝺa
houerꝼ ꝼ ꞇ ꞇ ꞇ ꞇ ꞇ
ꞇ ꞇ ꝼ ꞇ ꞇ ꞇ ꞇ ꞇ
ꞇ ꞇ ꞇ io nmek ꝼ ꞇ ꞇ uꝛimꝼo habe... ꞇ a ꝛ ꞇ e ꞇ e mc um ꞇ ꞇ tradiꞇ o
ꞇ ꞇ ꞇ lmuꝼll ꞇ ꞇ ꞇ noꞁ e ꞇ r... io

FIGURE 1.2. (*Top*) Oslac's charter. (*Bottom*) Offa's confirmation to Oslac's charter. (Chichester Cap I/17/2. Reproduced with permission.)

33

duties were clarified by the king who made it his business to build, fortify, and defend an earthwork which established his western boundary. Offa also initiated the Mercian tradition of reserving to the king certain basic judicial powers. In so doing, he solidified the king's position as the source of law and justice "by God's grace." Figure 1.3 charts the royal itineraries, as attested by references in surviving charters, during reigns of the Mercian kings. Offa's movements, for example, begin in Canterbury where he could claim at the archbishop's hand his God-given right to rule and illustrate his attempts to unify his kingdom by means of the regal presence.

The Uses of Literacy

Anglo-Saxon notions about kingship were closely tied to the literate products of king lists, royal genealogy, and royal legislation, which were themselves intertwined in the Germanic mind:

> Genealogies and king-lists are . . . associated with early medieval royal legislation. . . . The ecclesiastical connexions of the early Germanic law-codes suggest that churchmen felt king-list and royal genealogies to be important mirrors of a king's right to rule. A king had a long line of royal predecessors: he belonged to a royal tradition. A king possessed an appropriately royal pedigree; therefore he was of royal blood. A king legislated; therefore he was a king.[14]

We have evidence that Offa used his professional scriptorium to help him assert his kingship through the production of genealogies and laws (in addition to the charters). Offa substantiated the claim of an early charter which described him as "sprung from the royal stock of the Mercians and made king by appointment of Almighty God" by having his genealogy compiled from available (probably Northumbrian) sources. The survival of the genealogy in a number of different manuscripts is strong indication that it was considered

[14] David N. Dumville, "Kingship, Genealogies and Regnal Lists," in P. H. Sawyer and I. N. Wood, ed., *Early Medieval Kingship* (Leeds: The University of Leeds, 1977), pp. 74–75.

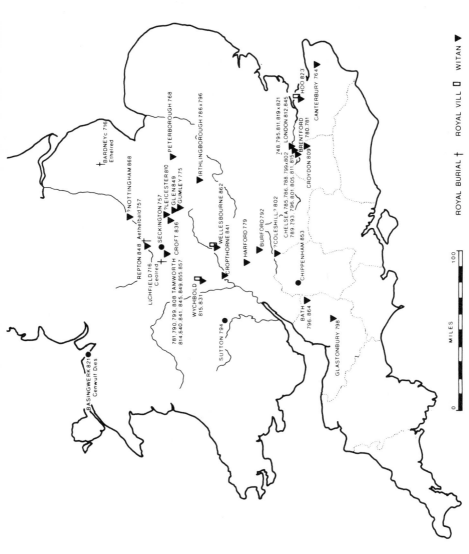

FIGURE 1.3. The itineraries of the kings of Mercia. (Reproduced with permission from David Hill, *An Atlas of Anglo-Saxon England* [Toronto: University of Toronto Press, 1981], p. 83.)

35

a very important document. Further, we have the testimony of contemporary authors that Offa was a lawmaker of note. Alfred, who drew so heavily on Mercian learned achievements, specifically acknowledges his debt to Offa's laws, which Alcuin praised as good, moderate, and chaste. "Alfred's law-book was accompanied not only by the Chronicle, but also by West Saxon king-list and genealogy."[15] Offa, then, began the English tradition of making permanently effable expressions of kingship through the codification of dynasties and legislation.

Offa also manipulated social convention to make good his claim to being king of all the English people. He increased his own dignity by making royal personages of his wife and son, both of whom joined him as witnesses to charters. His wife, Queen Cyneðryð, was further dignified with her own coinage; she is the only consort ever to appear on an English coin. Through a great deal of bloodshed and coercion, Offa was able to secure the succession of his son Ecgfrið (who reigned only 141 days). He went so far as to have Ecgfrið consecrated king in his own time; the first recorded anointing of an English king added the official sanction of the church to Mercian hegemony. Offa maximized his own security by giving his daughters in marriage to the kings of Wessex and Northumbria.

An important measure of Offa's greatness was the respect he was accorded outside of England. He carried on an extended, friendly correspondence with Charlemagne, and Charlemagne was ever careful to treat Offa as a peer, even suggesting the marriage of his son Charles to one of Offa's daughters. "Even at Rome Offa seemed a real, though inscrutable, force in the international world."[16] Offa was able to attract the first papal legation to England since the formation of the English church, and presided personally over the synod of southern bishops which welcomed the legation. Although it is possible that it was the papal legates who anointed Ecgfrið, it

[15] Patrick Wormald, "*Lex Scripta* and *Verbum Regis:* Legislation and Germanic Kingship," in Sawyer and Wood, *Early Medieval Kingship*, p. 134.

[16] Stenton, *Anglo-Saxon England*, p. 215.

is certain that Offa took the occasion of their visit to argue for a Mercian metropolitan see.

As extensive as Offa's power was, rebellion in some portion of his kingdom was an inevitable aspect of hegemony. There were certain to be periodic challenges of an overlord's authority. Trouble in Kent would present a further complication: The archbishop of Canterbury, the head of the southern church, might join, or at least be sympathetic toward, a challenge against Mercian authority. Opposition from the church, even lack of cooperation, would make an overlord's position untenable. Iænberht did in fact constitute such a real threat; his signature is conspicuously absent in some charters where it might have been expected or desired. At any rate, Offa was successful in arguing that the southern church had grown too large to be administered efficiently by a single archbishop. Pope Hadrian acceded reluctantly, and in A.D. 788 Hygeberht received the pallium which made him Archbishop of Lichfield, the peer of Canterbury and York. In the same year Hygeberht witnessed a grant by Offa of land *in Kent*, something Iænberht might well have refused to do.

MERCIAN ENGLAND

Cultural achievement during the period of Mercian supremacy reflected the accumulative effect of 80 years of relative peace under Æðelbald and Offa, although there is understandably greater evidence of it during Offa's reign. Archeological excavations indicate that this was a period of extensive fortification and development of towns. For example, Offa defined the western frontier of his kingdom by initiating the construction of a 70-mile defensive earthwork, which has been compared to the pyramids as far as expenditure of effort. At about the same time a dyke was built to protect *Tomtun*, the ancient royal residence of Mercian kings, making it what the Anglo-Saxons termed a *worðig*. Thus, beginning in Offa's reign, Mercian kings held court in the royal city of *Tomworðig* (modern

Tamworth) at Christmas and Easter. The several hundred coins that survive from Offa's reign evidence an extensive and profitable administrative structure. Their beauty and integrity proclaim a king of substance.

The Synod of Clovesho in A.D. 747 required that priests know the mass, the rite of baptism, the creed, and the Lord's Prayer in English. That requirement helps account for the impulse among the Anglo-Saxon literati to compile Latin–Old English glossaries and to make interlinear glosses to religious texts. Since the church played a crucial role in the establishment of the Anglo-Saxon monarchy, kings would understandably commission the production of deluxe Bibles and psalters for use at state occasions. Any Mercian king would want to have a copy of Bede's history, the text that asserts the ascendancy of the Mercian dynasty by A.D. 731. The *British Museum Cotton Tiberius C. ii* is a manuscript of Bede known to have been copied in the south during the reign of Offa. Alcuin in one of his letters sent Offa to look up a passage in his copy of the history; Offa was an interested user of books, not a mere patron of literacy.

Secular literature also flourished at this time. The bulk of Anglo-Saxon poetry, although it survives in late West Saxon copies, was composed in Mercian times. The poetic koine has a distinctly Mercian substratum; Cynewulf, the only major Old English poet we know by name, has long been accepted as a Mercian, probably from Lichfield. The interest that the authors of the *Beowulf* and *Widsith* poems showed in the continental King Offa (from whom Offa the Great labored to demonstrate descent) prompted no less an Anglo-Saxonist than Professor Whitelock to suggest that they were composed during Offa's reign, if not at his court. Every aspect of Mercian cultural development was used by the Mercian kings to celebrate the glory of the social institution of kingship. Powerful kings enabled the Anglo-Saxon peoples to build a society and culture based on peace rather than constant intertribal hostility. Because culture and its benefits derived from the overlords, eighth-century culture, throughout England, was Mercian culture; eighth-century literacy especially was Mercian literacy.

Mercian England

The power of the Mercian hegemony was at its apex when Offa died in A.D. 796. Cenwulf (A.D. 796–821), Offa's distant relative, inherited the kingdom of Mercia—not the kingdom of the South English. Kent had revolted; the kings of Northumbria and Wessex whom Offa had allied to him through marriage were dead. After 2 years of bitter struggle, Cenwulf was able to subdue the Kentish and establish his younger brother Cuðred as king of Kent. Cenwulf resumed direct Mercian rule of Kent upon his brother's death in A.D. 807. Although Cenwulf and his successors never attained the position of an Æðelbald or an Offa, it would be a mistake to underestimate their power. Until the Mercian defeat by the West Saxons in A.D. 825, they were certainly the strongest and most influential of the southern kings. Cenwulf ruled supreme in the southeast (East Anglia, Essex, Kent, and Sussex); and, although he never claimed control of Wessex, he also was never subject to the West Saxons. He enjoyed the distinct advantage of having two friendly southern archbishops—his own metropolitan at Lichfield and Æðelheard of Canterbury. Offa had worked hard to secure the favor of Æðelheard, granting him a large estate in Middlesex. Æðelheard was so clearly Mercia's man that he was forced to flee Kent during the years of revolt. With Canterbury on friendly terms, Cenwulf had little need of a Mercian archbishopric, and he offered to reunite the southern church if the pope would in return move the archiepiscopal see to London (which had long been a Mercian city and remained one until the Danish invasions). The pope knew he was dealing with no peer of Charlemagne. When he conferred the pallium on Æðelheard, he confirmed on Canterbury its ancient primacy over all of the southern church. In A.D. 803, a synod of the English bishops at Clovesho followed suit and declared the archbishopric of Lichfield invalid. Mercian kings were again vulnerable to hostility from Canterbury, as Cenwulf would soon discover. Æðelheard's successor was his archdeacon Wulfred, whose pontificate of 27 years saw the end of Mercian domination of Kent. At first the relationship between Wulfred and Cenwulf was cordial. Cenwulf made generous grants of land to Wulfred, "my archbishop," and Wulfred was available to witness Cenwulf's charters. However, the two quarreled, with the notable result that Cenwulf's steady flow of charters ceased until a settlement was reached in A.D. 821! Cenwulf was powerful enough to impose a settlement upon Wulfred, but his generosity indicates his knowledge of the extent of his vulnerability.

THE DECAY OF MERCIAN AUTHORITY

Cenwulf spent the last years of his reign attempting to reestablish the glory of Mercia by conducting an unsuccessful (and unpopular) campaign of expansion against the Welsh. In the end, Cenwulf's policy aided only the West Saxon cause; while the Mercians were weakening themselves through overambition, the West Saxons were consolidating their position in the southwest. Ceolwulf (A.D. 821–823) followed Cenwulf's example and declared himself "king of the Mercians and the Kentish." In Ceolwulf, the Mercian royal dynasty, which Offa took such pains to declare, ended; Beornwulf, his successor (A.D. 823–825) had signed two of Cenwulf's charters as a mere *dux*, "ealdorman." "It was now the turn of Mercia to suffer the fate of kingdoms ruled by non-royal stocks."[17] Beornwulf's southeastern dominance was limited to control of Essex, Kent, and Middlesex, although he still enjoyed the important favor of Canterbury. In A.D. 825, Beornwulf presided over the last of the 21 ecclesiastical councils which had typified, and substantiated, the Mercian claims to be the rulers of Britain. In the same year, Egbert of Wessex overwhelmed the Mercians and began the policies that would establish the West Saxon dynasty. Wiglaf (A.D. 830–839) was the last Mercian king to challenge West Saxon supremacy significantly. Even though Wiglaf was temporal lord over only the original kingdom of Mercia (plus London and Middlesex), the tradition of Mercian control over the southern church was so strong that Wiglaf could

[17] D. J. V. Fisher, *The Anglo-Saxon Age c. 400–1042* (London: Longman, 1973), p. 200.

attract the archbishop of Canterbury and 11 other bishops to sign his charter of A.D. 836. Mercia certainly no longer controlled the south, but she could not but continue to be a prominent influence in southern politics. Thus, the notion of kingship on which the West Saxons modeled their monarchy was a Mercian cultural product. Just as importantly, the English intellectual establishment was a Mercian cultural artifact; Mercians would continue to dominate English literacy until the time of Alfred (c. A.D. 875).

STUDYING THE CONSEQUENCES OF MERCIAN LITERACY

The development of English literacy, then, belongs to the period of the supremacy of the Mercian kings. The history of that Mercian hegemony is the history of the institutionalization of the powers of the Mercian kings. The church played a dual role in that process. In the first place, the church, especially by the presence of its chief prelates, confirmed that the kings, who signed their names "with the Holy Cross," were in fact king "by divine dispensation," "by the gift of God." Were it not for the written word, those attestations would have been as ephemeral as memory. The greater role that lettered churchmen played was in the production of written products—charters, chronicles, histories, genealogies, laws, epic songs—which gave wordly flesh to a king's claims. The literate community not only served the king; it was dependent on him. In violent times, literacy is a luxury, albeit a useful one. Only a very powerful overlord could produce a social climate that enabled the pursuit of letters and could grant the economic base (land) necessary for maintaining a community of scholars. A king's support, at least in a large measure, was politically motivated; the productions of the communities he supported would naturally reflect his politics. "The affairs of church and state were in fact interdependent, and no king or bishop of the eighth century would have understood an argument which tried to show that ecclesiastical legislation, or the protection of ecclesiastical interests, was a matter for churchmen alone."[18] A text produced anywhere in southern England during the period of Mercian supremacy must be considered in some respects a Mercian text.

The data for this study of the earliest examples of English literacy have been gathered from the manuscripts produced during the Mercian hegemony and the years that preceded the rise of the West Saxon hegemony. An attempt has been made to include every English word written in southern England before A.D. 900. The sources trace a development from the use of occasional English words— names and glosses—in Latin texts to complete interlinear glosses and full prose passages; that is, a development from experimentation to fluency in literacy. The longest and most extensive text is the interlinear gloss to the *Vespasian Psalter* (c. A.D. 825). Philologists early discovered the gloss to reflect an extremely consistent phonological system; consequently, the *Vespasian Psalter* has long been the focus of the study of Mercian Old English. Fortunately, a set of closely interrelated Latin–Latin and Latin–Old English glossaries (the *Epinal, Erfurt,* and *Corpus* texts) supply extensive data for the beginning of the Mercian period. Charters offer a continuous record of written English in contemporary documents whose date and provenience (at least the location of the grants) are well established. Used cautiously and with the understanding that they are more likely to reflect the language of the dominant political force than that of the locale of the grant, they enrich the study of English during the Mercian hegemony. The remaining texts provide, as it were, a range of informants.

The official relationship between the literate community and the kings is clear, but unfortunately we know little about the composition of the professional learned class, the immediate source of the texts of this study. We do know that in early Anglo-Saxon times religious communities tended to be geographically heterogeneous:

[18] Stenton, *Anglo-Saxon England*, p. 238.

Studying the Consequences of Mercian Literacy

> That the clergy felt their vows and spiritual relations to be a much
> more real tie than mere nationality must have led to the elimination
> of provincial feeling among them. A Mercian priest was free of all
> the churches. A Mercian or West Saxon prelate might rule at Can-
> terbury; the bishop of East Anglia might be a Kentish man, and a
> South Saxon might rule at Rochester.[19]

Of the seven archbishops of Canterbury between A.D. 731 and 836,
for example, four were Mercians, one was a Saxon, and only two
were Kentish. What is again important is the fact that *kings* made
bishops, established and maintained religious houses, and had the
prerogative of removing support. Kings would, whenever possible,
place family and reliably friendly prelates in positions of honor and
authority. Thus the geographical provenience of a manuscript is of
questionable interest; its being written at Canterbury cannot assure
that it was written by a Kentsman. As the whole scholarly tradition
of the eighth and early ninth century developed under nearly exclusive
Mercian domination, we can expect that a text written in Canterbury
will exhibit Mercian influence. Literacy and politics were no more
separable in Anglo-Saxon England than were church and state.
Literate texts, as in the case of the charters, were often explicitly
political acts. Such texts as histories, laws, and genealogies were
politically motivated; no text could be apolitical. Of the uses of
writing detailed in this chapter, Lévi-Strauss has this to say:

> And when we consider the first uses to which writing was put, it
> would seem quite clear that it was connected first and foremost with
> power: it was used for inventories, catalogues, censuses, laws and
> instructions; in all instances, whether the aim was to keep a check
> on material possessions or on human beings, it is evidence of the
> power exercised by some men over other men and over worldly
> possessions.[20]

---

[19] Bishop Stubbs, *Constitutional History of England*, vol. 1, 6th ed.
(Oxford: Oxford University Press, 1897), p. 243.
[20] Georges Charbonnier, ed., *Conversations with Claude Lévi-Strauss*
(London: Jonathan Cape, 1969), p. 30.

2

RECONSTITUTING THE SOUNDS OF OLD ENGLISH

PEAKERS and spellers of Modern English might not readily understand how early Anglo-Saxon texts can provide the means of studying the pronunciation of early Old English. Our system of conventionalized spelling completely masks spoken variation. The written *out*, for example, covers an amazing range of pronunciations—[əᵘ ~ ɑᵘ ~ aᵘ ~ æᵘ ~ ɛᵘ ~ ɛːᵒ ~ eːᵒ ~ eːü] in the vowel, not to mention some of the possible variants for the final consonant (cluster?), [ʔt ~ ʔ]. We accept as "natural" what might well amaze us: It occurs to none of us (except for a few writers of literary dialect) to attempt to reflect in our written language the variation that occurs in different social, regional, and stylistic contexts.

The situation was radically different in early eighth-century Anglo-Saxon England. To begin with, English had not been widely written. The runic alphabet, a Germanic invention, was already in use, but its currency was limited. Runic writing was largely reserved for ritual practices. On the other hand, the Christian clergy were not only literate (in Latin), they championed the role that widespread literacy could play in the conversion of the English peoples. As Christianity became the official religion of the realm, kings had at their disposal an established social class already versed in the extensive uses of literacy. As the need and desire to write English developed, it was only natural that Anglo-Saxon religious would adapt the Latin alphabet to the task of recording the sounds of English. As it happens, we assimilated a world-view in the process of borrowing an alphabet; we learned what kinds of things can be done in the act of making a permanent record of speech. It may

46

have been curiosity that led to the first experiment, but it was utility that impelled the expanded use of written speech. The marriage of church and state determined that we would use the Latin alphabet.

Traditionally, the Roman alphabet had been applied more or less phonetically in the representation of spoken Latin. Certain spellings had indeed become conventional over time, but a strong set of orthographic–phonological correspondences had developed. With minor modifications (the addition of ð and runic þ for the dental fricatives, for example), Roman literate habit could become English second nature. The result is that the earliest texts are much like broad transcription in the International Phonetic Alphabet. In the absence of the weight of traditional spellings, scribes represent their own individual speech idiosyncratically, though faithfully. We do not find speaker-to-speaker (text-to-text) differences masked by received spellings; we find variation. Further, we can hope for the kind of data we get from the naive speller of American English who does not spell *water* and *butter* phonemically with a medial *t*, but records the [d]-like quality of the flap. We can be certain that early writers would record all systematic linguistically significant contrasts, but we know that linguistic significance does not reside exclusively in contrast. It is not unreasonable to suppose that Anglo-Saxon scribes also (unconsciously) recorded their phonetic habits. The important (and open) question is: How concrete or abstract was the correspondence between the phonological system of Old English and its orthographic representation? A thorough examination of the data will assist us in answering this question. We need only assume that orthographic consistency was motivated by linguistic reality.

Because a language changes at a rather slow rate, a scribe will not depart radically from the set of phonological–orthographic correspondences that he learned from his teachers. As a result, linguistic innovation may be masked in the historical record, as spelling conventions begin to develop. Oral habits, however, are apt to slip into a scribe's writing; hence the importance of consistent variations in spelling. The same conservative scribe may also provide data of another sort—hypercorrections. When sounds have begun to fall together in a language, their orthographic representations tend to be confused. It is difficult, if not impossible, for a scribe to monitor these variations, which makes them extremely important to the historical linguist. Orthographic systems can, of course, vary independently of the spoken language. If, however, an orthographic variation can be tied to a known historical change (attested by comparative data, etc.), it is reasonable to assume that the orthographic variation reflects, within the stated limits, that sound change.

THE SOUNDS AND SPELLINGS OF EARLIEST ENGLISH

Early Anglo-Saxon scribes used the following symbols to represent the stressed vowels of Old English:[1] *i, e, æ* (variously spelled *ae,* ẹ, and *æ*), *y, oe, a, o, u, ea* (also spelled *æa*), *eo,* and *io.* Vowel quantity was (irregularly) indicated by doubling the vowel. On the basis of comparative studies with other Old Germanic languages, we reconstruct a vowel system that coincides remarkably well with the orthographic system of the earliest English texts (the *Epinal, Erfurt,* and *Corpus Glossaries*). It is a vowel system that contrasts front with back vowels; high, mid, and low vowels; and front rounded with front spread vowels (each symbol represents a contrastively long and short pair):

	Front		Back
	Round	Spread	
high	*y*	*i*	*u*
mid	*oe*	*e*	*o*
low		*æ*	*a*

[1] Spellings will be indicated by italics in order to distinguish them from underlying representations and phonetic transcriptions.

48

The Sounds and Spellings of Earliest English

We also reconstruct a set of three diphthongs—*æa* (usually spelled *ea*), *eo*, and *io*. Subsequent changes in the language (especially the tendency of long vowels to be raised) lead us to suspect that long and short vowels differed in quality as well as quantity. Specifically, we think that long front vowels tended to be fronter and higher (more peripheral) than their quantitatively short counterparts. The short front vowels of English have been remarkably stable over the past 1000 years. There is no reason to suppose that the following Old English words were pronounced much differently from their modern counterparts (given in broad phonetic transcriptions):

pitt [pɪt]   *sett* [sɛt]   *blæc* [blæk]   *Offa* [ɔfə]

Of these vowels, [æ] has historically been the most volatile, moving around in the low front region, and occasionally into the low central region—as it continues to do in modern social and regional dialects: [glɑd ~ glad ~ gla·d ~ glæd ~ glɛːəd ~ gliəd]. Old English /a/ was a low back sound (details follow), pronounced [ɒ] as it is in some dialects today, OE god = modern [gɒd]. Old English short *o* and short *u* were probably nonperipheral as well—[ɔ] and [ʊ]—since their modern reflexes are much lowered sounds: *Offa* [ɔfə ~ ɒfə] *even* [ɑfə], and *nut* [nʌt]. Given these trends of historical development, we can suppose a system of vowel contrasts in earliest Old English something like that charted in Figure 2.1 (length marked with a colon; rounded vowels in parentheses and pronounced in roughly the same position as their spread equivalents). There was general confusion of the spelling of the unstressed vowels; that confusion is probably an indication that unstressed vowels were weakening to schwa-like values. As there was also widespread confusion in the spelling of the off-glide element of the diphthongs, we might suppose that those elements too were in the process of being weakened to central vowels. The digraph spellings *ea* (an Old English orthographic convention for *æa*), *eo*, and *io* (often spelled *iu* earlier) clearly point to backing off-glides which developed over time into centralizing off-glides. The height of the first element may have had a minor conditioning effect on the height of the centralized off-

49

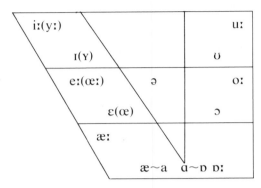

FIGURE 2.1. The unit vowels of early Old English.

glide, as the spellings suggest. Widespread confusion in the spelling of the second element of the digraph suggests that these diphthongs can reasonably be transcribed [æə, ɛə, ɪə]. In the body of this text, spellings will be italicized. Underlying forms will be printed in roman letters between phonemic slashes; the content of the slashes will reflect *spellings,* since traditional treatments of Old English discuss sounds in terms of spellings. The best guess at the phonetic reality that motivated spellings will be printed within phonetic brackets. A macron indicates quantitative length in spellings and underlying forms:

Spelling	Underlying form	Phonetic form
ēa	/ǣa/	[æːə]
ea	/æa/	[æə]
ēo	/ēo/	[eːə]
eo	/eo/	[ɛə]
īo	/īo/	[iːə]
io	/io/	[ɪə]

The quantitatively long diphthongs were a development of Germanic diphthongs; the short diphthongs were an Old English allophonic innovation.

The Sounds and Spellings of Earliest English

Certain categorical, allophonic alternations are well attested (and generally accepted) as a part of the earliest Old English phonological system (the language of the *Epinal, Erfurt,* and *Corpus Glossaries*):

(1) Short *æ* and *a* alternated[2] in complementary distribution, with *a* conditioned by a nasal consonant or a back vowel in the following syllable:[3]

> *dæg* (day, nominative singular) but *dagas* (days, nominative plural)
> *dæges* (day's) but *dagum* (days, dative plural)
> *mann* (man)

Since the vowel spelled *a* by early scribes conditioned *a* rather than *æ* in the previous syllable, *a* must have itself been a back vowel.

In a related phenomenon, we find only *a* (never *æ*) before certain velar (back) consonants and consonant groups:

> *awel* (hook) and *gesawen* (seen)
> *all* and *half* (identical with modern English spellings)

The process is referred to as the "retraction of *æ*" in philological terms; a generative phonologist would say that *a* is derived from an underlying *æ*.

(2) The front vowels (long and short) underwent a conditioned diphthongization during the Primitive Old English period, which antedates the first texts. The diphthongization process, known traditionally as "breaking," produced early Old English diphthongal allophones of short *æ, e,* and *i,* and long *e* and *i* in the following environments:[4]

---

[2] The terms *alternate* and *alternation* are used in this study to refer specifically to categorical complementary distribution; *vary* and *variation* refer to noncategorical, but statistically predictable, subphonemic distribution.

[3] Examples are frequently taken from A. Campbell, *Old English Grammar* (Oxford: Oxford University Press, 1959).

[4] Long *æ* had merged with long *e* in all varieties of Old English.

/__χ (spelled *c*, *g*, and *h*)	*meaht* (might)
	eoh (horse)
	tiohhian (consider)
/__r plus a consonant	*heard* (hard)
	sweord (sword)
	iorre (anger)
/__w (except for *æ* as above)	*hweowol* (wheel)
	niowul (prostrate)

A number of further developments distinguish the allophony of the later Mercian texts, notably the *Vespasian Psalter:*

(3) Earlier *a* is written *o* when it occurs before a nasal consonant— *monn* (man), *lond* (land), *gongan* (go).

(4) The long and short diphthongs that had developed before the velar spirant (and *l* and *r* plus [χ]) became monophthongs once again (in a process called "smoothing")—*mæht* (might), *merg* (marrow), *feh* (money), etc.

(5) The long and short diphthongs[5] *io* and *eo* merged—*lēoht* = *līoht* (light), *meox* = *miox* (manure).

(6) Short *æ* was regularly raised to a vowel spelled *e*, probably [ε]—*deȝ* (day), *feder* (father), in a sound change known as the "second fronting."

(7) A new set of short diphthongs developed from front vowels when they occurred in syllables preceding a back vowel: *i* and *e* became *io* and *eo* (except before the smoothing environment of *χ*)—*weoruld* (world), *piosan* (peas). This diphthongization has traditionally been called "velar (or back) umlaut."

(8) Stressed short *a* (retracted *æ*) in such words as *dagas* was fronted to a vowel spelled *æ*, yielding [dægas] which underwent diphthongization (as described immediately above) to *deagas*.

Anglo-Saxon scribes were very consistent in their transcription of the accented vowels of Old English. There is no scribal confusion

[5] For convenience, length in diphthongs will be marked by the macron.

among the contrastive vowels. The allophones of items (1) and (2) above are represented with consistent regularity in even the earliest of texts; these allophonic alternations are known to have been produced by prehistoric sound changes. Although items (3)–(6) are spelled regularly (are alternations) in late texts (especially the *Vespasian Psalter*), scribes varied their spellings of the same developments in the earliest texts. That is, the Old English word for *man* would fluctuate between *monn* and *mann* in the *Corpus Glossary*, for example. The treatment of such variation in spelling, and the phonological system it may represent, is the crucial issue confronted by this book. A brief survey of the history of the linguistic study of Old English texts will contextualize the study of scribal variation and help justify the methods of inquiry.

THE STUDY OF EARLY ENGLISH PHONOLOGY

The earliest philological investigations of Old English were detailed studies of individual texts.[6] They are little more than catalogues of the early English developments of each reconstructed primitive Germanic form, but they are exhaustive. Consider the following typical description (abbreviated for easier reading) of the sounds that developed from West Germanic *a* (the subject of Chapters 3 and 4 of this study):

WG *a* appears as *æ* (*ae*), *a, o, ea, e, eo*.
1. It appears as *æ:*
    a) in monosyllabic words, representing the normal independent development of the vowel: *Huaet-, -haed;*
    b) before a double consonant in *Aebbæ;*

      . . .

[6] For example, Edward Miles Brown, *Die Sprache der Rushworth Glossen zum Evangelium Matthäus und der merische Dialect* (I. Vokale) (Göttingen: W. Fr. Kästner, 1891); ibid., *The Language of the Rushworth Gloss to the Gospel of Matthew and the Mercian Dialect* (Part II) (Göttingen: W. Fr. Kästner, 1892); Ferdinand Dieter, *Uber Sprache und Mundart der ältesten englischen Denkmäler* (Göttingen: G. Calvör, 1885); Rudolf Zeuner, *Die Sprache des Kentischen Psalters* (Helle: Max Niemeyer, 1881).

53

2. It appears as *a:*
   a) before a single cons. followed by a velar vowel: *Badu-, Hadu-* (as for the exceptions *Beadu* and *Peada,* see § 1.4.d, § 18);
   b) sometimes before a geminated cons. followed by a velar vowel: *Acca, Acha*—Notice the absence of breaking, *Adda, Basso, Padda;*
   c) sometimes before nasals: *Anna, Andhun, Iaruman, Colman;*

   . . .

3. It appears as *o:*
   sometimes before nasals: *Tondberct, Tondheri, Caedmon, Tilmon.*[7]

Even the most minor of deviations is noted if not in some manner "explained." In fact, the major directions of the early sound changes are often obscured as simple opening statements to be followed by pages of exceptions. Sounds were treated as individuals with little regard either to the overall pattern of the system or to internal systematic alternations within it. Because the neogrammarian approach emphasized the regularity of language change, a manuscript, like the *Vespasian Psalter,* with perfectly consistent orthography assumes pride of place in the philological tradition. The dialect of the scribe of the Psalter became *the* Mercian dialect. The richness of the data of other texts, however, was an embarrassment to scholars committed to a theory of perfectly regular sound change. Dialect mixture and analogy were heralded as the forces that produced the Old English profusion of variation. It was from these early collections of data that such men as Luick, Sievers, and Sweet— the first great synthesizers in English historical linguistics—built their grammars of Old English. Compare Sievers's treatment of West Germanic **a:*

49. In an originally closed syllable, wherever special circumstances do not prevent, short *a* is regularly converted into *æ: dæg,* . . .
50. In an originally open syllable the Germ. *a* appears sometimes as *a,* sometimes as *æ:*
    1) *a* regularly occurs when the following syllable contains one

---

[7] Hilmer Ström, *Old English Personal Names in Bede's History* (Lund: Hakan Ohlsson, 1939), pp. 91–92.

of the guttural vowels, *a, o, u*. Thus *dæg* has nom. plur. *dagas*, . . .

52. The changes undergone by original *a* in cases not included under the foregoing are as follows:

    1) before nasals it becomes *o* . . .

    2) it undergoes breaking to *ea* before *r* and *l* combinations, and before *h*; . . .[8]

The profound debt of modern Anglo-Saxon scholarship to these pioneer efforts can nowhere more clearly be seen than in Alistair Campbell's standard reference work *Old English Grammar*, which is little more than a careful summary of 100 years of neogrammarian research. The importance of Campbell's work to contemporary Anglo-Saxonists is also poignant testimony to the field's general resistance to innovations in linguistic science.

Structural linguists worked extensively with the neo-grammarian accounts of Old English while focusing their efforts on the best attested, and most regular, variety—late West Saxon. Because the emphasis of structuralist analysis was synchronic, phonemic description succeeded in producing clear accounts of the overall contrastive patterns of West Saxon.[9] The diachronic details of which sounds had split and merged since West Germanic times were sensibly left as a matter more appropriate to historical accounts. Although contemporary phonologists might argue about the autonomous status of phonemes, the universally accepted account of Old English vowel allophony was worked out by Brunner, Hockett, and Kuhn. Kuhn's work merged the concerns of philology and phonemic analysis. He worked at placing the profusion of orthographic variation of the early texts into the context of evolving vowel systems.[10] To do so,

[8] Eduard Sievers, *An Old English Grammar* (New York: AMS Press, 1970), pp. 31–34.

[9] See, for example, Karl Brunner, "The Old English Vowel Phonemes," *English Studies* 34 (1955): 247–251; S. Chatman, "The *a/æ* Opposition in Old English," *Word* 14 (1958): 224–236; C. Hockett, "The Stressed Syllabics of Old English," *Language* 35 (1959): 575–597.

[10] Sherman M. Kuhn, "The Dialect of the Corpus Glossary," *PMLA* 54 (1939): 1–19 and "On the Syllabic Phonemes of Old English," *Language* 37 (1961): 522–538.

he directed his effort toward identifying patterns within data that were otherwise being dismissed as "free variation." Kuhn accommodated his methods to fit the needs of the data, and the variable state of the language in the *Corpus Glossary* was better suited to an analysis more philological than phonemic in its orientation. His analysis of variation as representing sound change in progress is in many ways the model for this investigation. Kuhn was also the only structuralist who attempted to describe all of the dialectal varieties of Old English and to present his descriptions in the light of historical developments during the Anglo-Saxon period. Because of its admirable economy, it is worth including here his account (which, he notes, "obviously owes something to Hockett") of the development of the vowels in Mercian Old English between A.D. 700 and the date of the *Vespasian Psalter* (A.D. 825):

| | Front vowels | | | | Back vowels | | Diphthongs | | Unaccented vowels | |
	Unround		Round							
High	/i/	[ɪ]	/y/	[ü]	/u/	[ʊ]	/io/	[ɪɒ, ɪɛ]		
	/ī/	[iː]	/ȳ/	[üː]	/ū/	[uː]	/īo/	[ɪɒː, ɪɛː]	[ɨ]	
Mid	/e/	[ɛ]	/œ/	[ö]	/o/	[ɒ]	/eo/	[ɛɒ]		
	/ē/	[eː]	/œ̄/	[öː]	/ō/	[oː]	/ēo/	[ɛɒː]	/ə/	
Low	/æ/	[æ, æ⊥]	/ɔ̃/	[ɔ̈]	/a/	[ɑ, ə]	/æa/	[æɑ, æɒ]		[ə]
	/ǣ/	[æː, ɛː]			/ā/	[ɑː]	/ǣa/	[æɑː, æɒː]		

[c. 700]

| | Front vowels | | | | Back vowels | | Diphthongs | | Unaccented vowels | |
	Unround		Round							
High	/i/	[ɪ]	/y/	[ü]	/u/	[ʊ]	/io/	[ɪɒ]		
	/ī/	[iː]	/ȳ/	[üː]	/ū/	[uː]	/īo/	[ɪɒː, ɪɛː]	[ɨ]	
Mid	/e/	[ɛ]	/œ/	[ö]	/o/	[ɒ]	/eo/	[ɛɒ, ɛə]		
	/ē/	[eː]	/œ̄/	[öː]	/ō/	[oː]			/ə/	
	/ɛ/	[æ⊥]			/ə/	[ɔ]	/ēo/	[ɛɒː, ɛəː]		
Low	/æ/	[æ]			/a/	[ɑ]	/æa/	[æɑ, æə]		[ə]
	/ǣ/	[æː, ɛɪ]			/ā/	[ɑː]	/ǣa/	[æɑː, æəː]		

[c. 825]

56

The Study of Early English Phonology

The incidence of /æ/ had been greatly reduced by the operation of the second fronting in the eighth century. Except in a few positions, e.g. before /h/ in *mæht*, [æ] had moved to [æ⊥] and was a new phoneme. The short /œ/ was a relic phoneme, having almost completely fallen together with /e/. The long / œ̄/ was more stable, but this also was beginning to unround. The incidence of /a/ had been reduced by the splitting off of /ɔ/ and by the combined operation of velar umlaut and the second fronting, which caused /a/ in open syllable followed by back vowel to become /æa/. The diphthong /io/ was by this time a relic, surviving only in velar-umlaut position (*nioman*, etc.). Breaking-/io/ had fallen together with /eo/. The long /īo/ was rapidly falling together with /ēo/.

3.1. /ɔ̄/ was no longer a phoneme, having unrounded to /e/ in *ende*, *wemman*, etc.

3.2. /ɛ/ is a misleading symbol for the new phoneme from the second fronting of /æ/ from Gmc. /a/. Phonetically, the sound must have been somewhere between [æ] and [ɛ], for in ME times it coalesced with the reflexes of /æ/, /ɔ/, and /a/, not with the reflex of Merc. /e/. It is spelled *e* too regularly in the Vespasian gloss to be regarded as an allophone of /æ/, from which Hockett correctly separates it. A few minimal pairs contrasting /e/ and /ɛ/ are probably concealed by the *e*-spelling: *wes* (imp. sg. of *bīon*) : *wes* (pt. 1 and 3 sg.), *cweð* (imp. sg. of *cweoðan*) : *cweð* (pt. 1 and 3 sg.), *bed* (nom. sg.) : *bed* (pt. 1 and 3 sg. of *biddan*), *hel* (nom. sg.) : *hel* (pt. 1 sg. of *helan*). Pairs to illustrate the distinction /æ/ ~ /ɛ/, which no one appears to question, are much rarer, but perhaps *æt* (prep.) : *et* (adv.) will serve.

3.3. /ɔ/ < Gmc. and Lat. /a/ before nasal is consistently written *o*, and Hockett rightly separates it from /a/. That /ɔ/ was no longer a mere positional variant in Merc. is indicated by the shape of Late Lat. borrowings in the Vespasian gloss: *plant, geplantade,* (?)*organe*, etc. Moreover, /ɔ/ can appear before a consonant other than a nasal; cf. *born* (pt. 3 sg. of *beornan*), *orn* (pt. 1 sg. of *eornan*). That /ɔ/ did not fuse with /o/ is indicated by its falling together with /a, æ, ɛ/ in ME.

3.4. In later Merc. of the tenth century, /œ, œ̄, io, īo/ fell together with /e, ē, eo, ēo/ respectively. In the late tenth and eleventh centuries, /eo, ēo, æa, ǣa/ monophthongized to /ö, ȫ, æ, ǣ/.[11]

In 1939, Marjorie Daunt had initiated a challenge to the traditional diphthongal interpretation of the short digraph spellings *ea, eo, io;*[12]

---

[11] Kuhn, "On the Syllabic Phonemes," pp. 524, 533–534.
[12] Marjorie Daunt, "Old English Sound Changes Reconsidered in Relation

no one has ever doubted that the long digraphs reflected diphthongal pronunciations. She suggested that the digraphs, following Celtic orthographic practices, represented front vowels allophonically influenced by following consonants. Subsequent scholarship has unanimously rejected this view.[13] Stockwell and Barritt, and later Hockett, reopened the issue, this time suggesting that the digraphs represented back, spread monophthongs.[14] The argument has not received currency among Anglo-Saxonists. Kuhn and Quirk pointed out its inadequacies and marshaled a compelling comparative and historical argument against the position.[15]

Generative linguists have made several attempts to deal with the Old English data.[16] The use of underlying forms and multistep derivations of crucially ordered rules has proved a great source of economy and generality in describing patterns of subphonemic al-

---

to Scribal Tradition and Practice," *Transactions of the Philological Society* 1939 (1940): 108–137.

[13] M. L. Samuels, "The Study of Old English Phonology,"— *Transactions of the Philological Society* 1952 (1953): 15–47; Sherman M. Kuhn and Randolph Quirk, "Some Recent Interpretations of Old English Digraphs," *Language* 29 (1953): 143–156.

[14] R. P. Stockwell and C. Barritt, "The Old English Short Diphthongs: Some Considerations," *Language* 31 (1955): 372–389; Charles F. Hockett, "The Stressed Syllabics of Old English," *Language* 35 (1959): 575–597.

[15] Sherman M. Kuhn and Randolph Quirk, "The Old English Digraphs: A Reply," *Language* 31 (1955): 390–401.

[16] For example, Bezalel Elan Dresher, "Old English and the Theory of Phonology," Ph. D. dissertation, University of Massachusetts, 1978, and "The Mercian Second Fronting: A Case of Rule Loss in Old English," *Linguistic Inquiry* 11 (1980): 47–73; S. J. Keyser, "Metathesis and Old English Phonology," *Linguistic Inquiry* 6 (1975): 377–411; Paul Kiparsky and Wayne O'Neil, "The Phonology of Old English Inflections," *Linguistic Inquiry* 7 (1976): 527–557; Roger Lass, "Palatals and Umlaut in Old English," *Acta Linguistica Hafniensia* 1 (1970): 25–30, and Roger Lass and John Anderson, *Old English Phonology* (Cambridge: Cambridge University Press, 1975); K. A. Robb, "Some Changes in Kentish Old English Phonology," *Lingua* 20 (1968): 177–186; K. Wagner, *Generative Grammatical Studies in the Old English Language* (Heidelberg: Carl Winter, 1969).

ternations. Bezalel Elan Dresher's work is especially noteworthy for its elegance and explanatory power. It is probably not a coincidence that the majority of generative treatments continue to deal with morphophonemic alternations in the extremely regular varieties—West Saxon Old English and the language of the ninth-century *Vespasian Psalter*. Many articles that undertake an analysis of Old English phonology concern themselves with very small segments of the complete system and seem driven to highly abstract solutions. For example, in "Palatals and Umlaut in Old English," Lass chooses to account for the entirely opaque (not predictable by conditioning environment) umlaut vowels ([y:, Y, œ:, œ]) with a synchronic umlauting rule (back vowels become front round vowels when they occur before high front segments) and a conditioning factor which never appears on the surface.[17] The abstract solution, while getting around one problem, completely misses a linguistically significant generalization about Old English phonology. I-umlaut is simply not a productive process in Old English; the sound change is complete in the earliest English texts. Further, counterexamples are abundant. One does not find umlaut of the stem vowel in such words as *bodig* or the weak verbs of Class II (*lufian, fandian, langian, þolian, wunian,* etc.) Lass's rule is good diachrony but unmotivated synchrony.

Descriptions of systematic homogeneity (such as structuralist and generativist linguists have produced) are the necessary and appropriate artifacts of the first stages of linguistic analysis. Not until the patterns of contrast and conditioned alternations have been established, can attention be turned to patterned variation—the stuff of language change. Recent variationist studies of contemporary sound changes in progress have concentrated on subphonemic, statistical predictability in data previously dismissed as nonanalyzable.

[17] Roger Lass, "Palatals and Umlaut in Old English," *Acta Linguistica Hafniensia* 1 (1970): 25–30.

2 Reconstituting the Sounds of Old English

CORRELATING VARIATION AND CHANGE

Weinreich, Labov, and Herzog's insistence, in "Empirical Foundations for a Theory of Language Change," on a theory that could accommodate structured heterogeneity has culminated in several contemporary studies of sound changes in progress. Labov's *Sociolinguistic Patterns,* especially, has demonstrated variation which is conditioned by grammatical, social, and stylistic factors. Of special interest is Labov, Yaeger, and Steiner's *A Quantitative Study of Sound Change in Progress* (1972). The authors present exhaustive evidence that linguistic structure does not presuppose homogeneity, and work at refining a model that can accommodate heterogeneity and thus make possible the study of sound change in progress:

> Within the theoretical model of a homogeneous speech community there are serious problems of conceptualizing change, and it is not surprising that those who wrote on historical linguistics within this framework rejected on *a priori* grounds the possibility of studying sound change in progress (Bloomfield 1933:365, Hockett 1958:457; Chomsky 1965:3). When we abandon the identification of structure with homogeneity, it is possible to construct a rational model of change and begin to observe it (Weinreich, Herzog, and Labov 1968:100–101). Our present outlook predicts orderly heterogeneity within the community, and we expect to find change in progress located within specific social groups.[18]

The authors succinctly answer the charge that what they are observing is something other than changes in progress:

> Some linguists continue to insist that sound change is basically unobservable, and that our reports are records of "dialect mixture" or "the propagation of a change" rather than the change itself (King 1969:119; Postal 1968:284). The general position that we have taken is that no useful distinction can be made between a change and its

[18] William Labov, Malcah Yaeger, and Richard Steiner, *A Quantitative Study of Sound Change in Progress* (Philadelphia: The U.S. Regional Survey, 1972), pp. 3–4.

60

propagation (Weinreich, Labov, and Herzog 1968) as long as we continue to consider language an instrument of communication. The language does not change if one man invents an odd form or develops an idiosyncrasy, even if people understand and evaluate his behavior; it does change when others adopt his idiosyncrasy and use it as a new social convention for communicating their intent. The presence or absence of *dialect mixture* is an empirical issue which can be detected in our data.[19]

The challenge of dialect mixture is based ultimately on a notion of dialect which is itself an unnecessary abstraction. It is more realistic to speak of a speech community which loosely shares a set of typical features but within which there are subsystems in competition. The second fronting, for example, is a feature of Mercian Old English. To admit this is not to admit that second fronting was uniformly implemented in the language of all of the members of the Mercian speech community. Its implementation would be evident as a wave moving through the community and variously affecting speakers and even intruding into other "dialects" (as the second fronting did into Kentish). Indeed, the data to be presented in this study are an examination of the progress of such waves (or isoglosses). If this sort of diffusion is to be termed "dialect mixture," then that term becomes meaningless, since such diffusion is one of the processes of the implementation of sound change. The term is more happily reserved for sporadic and nonconditioned intrusions of nonnative forms, and its presence is empirically verifiable. However, once the diffusion becomes conditioned and predictable (even variably predictable), it is a viable force and no longer foreign.

Current interest in variation is enabling a new generation of linguists to turn their attention from what Anderson has termed *diachronic correspondences*[20] to closer study of the mechanisms of phonetic change. Historical Germanic philology which began as a close attention to detail has come full circle. The energy of our

[19] Ibid., pp. 6–7.
[20] Henning, Anderson, "Diphthongization," *Language* 48 (1972): 11–50.

philological predecessors derived from the discovery of the regularity of sound change; ours, from the correlation of patterns in the ubiquitous variation of living languages to the processes of linguistic change. Some scholars, of course, maintained an interest in phonetic change; Chadwick and Kuhn are notable among Anglo-Saxonists.[21]

In "Empirical Foundations for a Theory of Language Change," Weinreich, Labov, and Herzog articulated under four general headings the theoretical problems to be considered in the study of language change: the transition problem, the constraints problem, the embedding problem, and the actuation riddle. This classification of problems will serve as a useful guide to the variationist analysis of Old English data.

The Transition Problem

This issue centers on the traditional questions of the regularity and gradualness of sound change. All of the changes evaluated in this study involve variation in a phonetic class of sounds. In addition, most have as at least one of their conditioning factors a phonetic environment—which is to say that the changes hold true to at least part of the neogrammarian hypothesis. The sound changes, while being regular, do not, however, proceed without exception. Wang has proposed, on the basis of his work with developments in Middle Chinese, that sound changes proceed not by phonetic entity but word by word.[22] The data presented in this study, especially the

---

[21] H. M. Chadwick, "Studies in Old English," *Transactions of the Cambridge Philological Society* 4 (1894–1899): 85–265; S. M. Kuhn, "The Dialect of the Corpus Glossary," *PMLA* 54 (1939): 1–9; ibid., "*e* and *æ* in Farman's Glosses," *PMLA* 60: 631–669; ibid., "On the Syllabic Phonemes of Old English," *Language* 37 (1961): 522–538; ibid., "On the Consonant Phonemes of Old English," *Philosophical Essays . . . in Honour of Herbert Dean Meritt*, 1968.

[22] William S-Y Wang and Chin-chuan Cheng, "Implementation of Phonological Change: The Shuand-feng Chinese Case," in *Papers from the Sixth*

data drawn from the *Vespasian Psalter*, adds evidence in support of Wang's hypothesis of lexical diffusion.

Is sound change abrupt or gradual? Several misleading answers to this question have been proposed, especially in cases where writers have been too ready to lump together all varieties of sound change and have failed to discriminate between the ways in which a sound change may be abrupt or gradual. There are at least four levels at which the rate of sound change should be considered: phonological, phonetic, lexical, and statistical. Change at the phonological level is necessarily abrupt. Additions of surface forms, underlying representations, loss or addition of variable or obligatory rules, etc., cannot be other than abrupt. Phonetic changes can be abrupt or gradual. The shift from [æ] to [e] might proceed along a continuum rather than being accomplished in a series of discrete jumps. The deletion of a segment, on the other hand, can hardly be gradual: Either the segment is there or it is lost. Changes may diffuse gradually through the lexicon, item by item or class by class, as Wang has suggested. Changes in rates of variation—that is, statistical changes—are probably gradual (all those observed in ongoing sound changes have been), but they are at least potentially abrupt.

The Constraints Problem

A strong theory of language change would predict the direction of sound change after having established a set of possible changes and having described the sorts of pressures that apply to languages in flux. No such theory, of course, exists. Some work has been done in characterizing the types of sound systems that exist in natural languages and in noting the sorts of changes that languages undergo. One could predict, for instance, that if i-umlaut produced

---

Regional Meeting of the Chicago Linguistic Society (Chicago: Chicago Linguistic Society, 1970), pp. 552–559.

mid front round vowels, it would also produce high front round vowels.

The Embedding Problem

At which of the possible levels of abstraction in the phonological system does a sound change take place? Again, it is efficacious to determine whether the answer to this question is the same for all stages of sound change. At completion, the effects of a sound change in the phonological system are very abstract indeed. Unless the alternations produced by the sound change continue to participate in morphophonemic alternations, the completed sound change results in reconstruction of underlying forms. At the stage of implementation, current linguistic theory would also interpret the change in abstract terms. Implementation must involve rule additions, losses, or reorderings. The problems confronted in describing the initiation of sound change are very troublesome. Do sound changes enter the phonological system through performance, or do even the first minor variations signal the addition of a variable rule? Some low-level phonetic changes obviously begin as performance variation. The quantitative vowel length alternation before voiced and voiceless consonants in Modern English is an example. These systematic phonetic alternations often, as in the case of vowel nasalization, become productive forces in the phonological system. Issues of this kind strike close to the heart of the competence–performance dichotomy, which has been attacked on several fronts.[23] Although such considerations are far beyond the scope of this study, it is worthwhile to record as faithfully as possible the beginnings of changes that appear to have originated in low-level phonetic alternations.

[23] See especially Paul Kiparsky, "Explanation in phonology," in *Goals of Linguistic Theory* (Englewood Cliffs, N.J.: Prentice-Hall, 1972), pp. 189–227, and David Stampe, "How I Spent My Summer Vacation," Ph.D. dissertation, University of Chicago, 1972.

Correlating Variation and Change

The Actuation Riddle

The reasons for languages changing when they do and in the direction they do remain a mystery, except under certain conditions of language contact. The data from this study offer an opportunity to monitor the diffusion, throughout a whole speech community, of linguistic features characterizing a politically dominant group.

Several basic assumptions are necessary to the variationist analysis of the early Old English texts and the eventual attempt to discuss the data in terms of the framework outlined earlier. First, one must subscribe to what Labov has called the uniformitarian principle. That is, languages have always been, as they are now, in states of flux. The forces causing languages to change and the mechanisms of change were the same in the past as they are today. Structured variability was as much a fact for Old English as it is for Modern English. Linguistic variability is often the raw material for language change. In other words, variation can be change seen synchronically; change can be variation viewed diachronically. Certainly, the data of this study cannot be controlled as tightly as that which is collected by trained linguists in the contemporary social setting. We cannot know who informants were, where they came from, how long they had lived where they wrote, or which social or stylistic registers their writing represents. Further, the data are sparse and do not represent a cross section of the speech community. Without exception, the manuscripts were written by members of the great religious houses or by people who by virtue of their learning had been in contact with the religious. Yet, if linguistically significant variation representative of sound changes in progress can be found in these texts, then that variation demands analysis. Real data produced by native informants are to be preferred over any reconstruction. Limited as they are, the data are a valuable glimpse into the beginnings of the English language and deserve to be analyzed by the best methods available.

THE SOURCES FOR THE STUDY OF
EARLY OLD ENGLISH

Since the earliest Anglo-Saxon texts are the "informants" for this study, it is necessary to know them as well as possible. The following chronological summary suggests the extent to which the data base developed during the first 200 years of literacy in English (major sources are listed in capital letters; more limited but still extensive ones are boldface):

A.D. 700–750—EPINAL, Blickling Glosses, Names, Charters
A.D. 750–800—ERFURT, CORPUS, **Charters,** Leyden Glossary
A.D. 800–850—VESPASIAN PSALTER, **Lorica Glosses** and **Prayer, Charters**
A.D. 850–900—**Bede Glosses, Charters,** Codex Aureus

A detailed analysis and roughly chronological listing of these sources follows. Unless otherwise noted, the data are taken from Sweet's *Oldest English Texts.*[24] In all cases, the readings reported here have been checked against the original manuscripts.

The Charters

The selection criteria for inclusion of charters is in keeping with this study's effort to consider all texts known or suspected to contain Mercian varieties of Old English. Thus all charters written under Mercian kings or kings under Mercian domination are included. A charter is considered genuine and contemporary on the basis of the best current scholarship.[25] A typical entry consists of the charter's

[24] Henry Sweet, ed., *The Oldest English Texts* (Oxford: Oxford University Press, 1885).

[25] Peter H. Sawyer, *Anglo-Saxon Charters: An Annotated List and Bibliography* (London: Butler & Tanner, 1968) has been an invaluable aid. It contains an exhaustive list of charters granting land or secular rights over land and includes complete summaries of scholarly opinion on date and

date, Birch listing number,[26] Sweet listing number, manuscript number, manuscript dating, grantor, and grantee. The dates of manuscripts are reported using conventional abbreviations, for example, "s. viii" for the eighth century, "s. viii¹" for the first half of the eighth century, "s. viii²" for the second half of the eighth century, "s. viii med." for the middle of the eighth century, "s. viii/ix" for the later eighth or early ninth century, and "s. viii–ix" for the eighth and ninth centuries. For convenience, an asterisk has been placed before all charters in which Kuhn found evidence of the influence of Mercian scriptoria.[27] The following list is roughly chronological.

732	(B-148, S-6) *Cotton Augustus ii. 91* (s. viii?). Æthelberht, king of Kent, to Dunn, priest and abbot.
736	(B-154, S-9) *Cotton Augustus ii. 3* (s. viii¹). Æthelbald, king of the Mercians, to Cyneberht, *comes*. (Worcs.)
*742	(B-162, S-17) Canterbury, DC., *Chart. Ant. M 363* (s. ix¹). Æthelbald, king of Mercia, to the Kentish churches.[28]
759	(B-187, S-10) *B. M. Add. Ch. 19, 789* (s. viii med). Eanberht, Uhtred, and Ealdred (underkings of the Hwicce) to Headda, abbot. (Gloucs.)

provenience. In the establishment of the fact that the charters included in this study are contemporary (if not original), Mr. Sawyer has the corroboration of Mr. N. R. Ker and Mr. T. A. M. Bishop. It should be noted, however, that modern scholarship has in the main merely supported the work of earlier scholars. For example, the only charters added to this list of Mercian charters not included in Dahl's work are those passed over by Sweet from whom Dahl selected his sources.

[26] The standard edition of Anglo-Saxon charters is Walter de Gray Birch, *Cantularium Saxonicum* (London: Whiting, 1885–1889).

[27] Sherman M. Kuhn, "The *Vespasian Psalter* and the Old English Charter Hands," *Speculum* 18 (1943): 468–469.

[28] The date of this charter gives misleading indication of the date of the appearance of Mercian letter forms. The document is authentic, but it is an authentic, faithful *copy* (c. A.D. 825). The language is archaic (c. A.D. 750); the letter forms are contemporary (c. A.D. 825).

767   (B-176, S-8) *B. M. Stowe Ch. 3* (s. viii²). Eardwulf, king of Kent, to Heaberht, abbot.

764 for 767   (B-201, S-11) *Cotton Augustus ii. 26* (s. viii²). Offa, king of Mercia, to Stithberht, abbot.

770   (B-203, S-13) Worcester, DC., *Additional MS. in safe* (s. viii²). Uhtred, *regulus* of the Hwicce, to Æthelmund, *minister*.

779   (B-230, S-14) *Cotton Augustus ii. 4* (s. viii²). Offa, king of Mercia, to Dudda, *minister*. (Gloucs.)

788   (B-254, S-18) Cant. DC., *Chart. Ant. M 340* (s. viii¹). Offa, king of Mercia, to Osberht. (Kent)

*793X796   (B-274, S-16). *B. M. Add. Ch. 19, 790* (s. viii/ix). Offa, king of Mercia, to Æðelmund. (Gloucs.)

*798   (B-289, S-19). *Cotton Augustus ii. 97* (s. vii/ix). Cenwulf, king of Mercia, to Oswulf. (Kent)

799   (B-293) *B. M. Stowe Ch. 7* (s. ?).[29] Cenwulf, king of Mercia, to Christ Church, Canterbury. (Kent)

801   (B-201, S-12) *Cotton Augustus ii. 27* (s. viii²). Pilheard's indorsement of *X*. (Middlesex)

803   (B-312, S-33) *Cant. Arch. C. I.*[30] Grant of Æthelheard.

*803   (B-310, S-46) *Cotton Augustus ii. 61*. Council at Clofesho abolishes the Archbishopric of Lichfield.

*805   (B-321, S-49) *B. M. Stowe Ch. 9* (s. ix¹). Cenwulf, king of Mercia, and Cuthred, king of Kent, to Wulfhard, priest. (Kent)

805   (B-319) *Cotton Augustus ii. 55* (s. ix¹). Æthelheard, archbishop of Canterbury, recovers land at Bishopsbourne, Kent.

*805X807   (B-318, S-34) *Cotton Augustus ii. 100* (s. ix¹). *Stowe 8* (s. ix¹). Cuðred to Æðelnoð.

---

[29] Even though Sawyer leaves the date of this "original" charter a question, F. M. Stenton in 1918 judged it an original. Modern scholarship supports Stenton's view (Sawyer, *Charters,* p. 111).

[30] Sawyer, *Charters,* does not include "charters" of a purely ecclesiastical nature, such as this and the following document. The date of these documents, however, has never been questioned.

*805X810	(B-330, S-37) *Cotton Augustus ii. 79* (s. ix[1]). Oswulf, *aldormonn*, and Boernthryth, his wife, to Christ Church.
808	(B-326, S-50) *Cotton Augustus ii. 98* (s. ix). Cenwulf, king of Mercia, to Eadwulf, *minister*. (Kent)
*811	(B-332, S-35) *Cotton Augustus ii. 47* (s. ix[1]). Wulfred, archbishop, to Christ Church. (Kent)
*811	(B335, S-51) *Cotton Augustus ii. 10* (s. ix[1]). Cenwulf, king of Mercia, to Wulfred, archbishop. (Kent)
811	(B-339) *Cotton Ch. viii. 31* (s. ix[1]). Cenwulf, king of Mercia, to Beornmod, bishop. (Kent)
*812	(B-341, S-52) *Cant. DC., Chart. Ant. C. 1278* (s. ix[1]). Cenwulf, king of Mercia, to Wulfred, archbishop. (Kent)
814	(B-343) *B. M. Harley Ch. 83 A. 1* (s. ix[1]?). Cenwulf, king of Mercia, to Swithnoth, his *comes*. (Kent)
*814	(B-348, S-53) *Cotton Augustus ii. 74* (s. ix[1]). Cenwulf, king of Mercia, to Wulfred, archbishop.
*815	(B-353, S-54) *B. M. Stowe Ch. 12* (s. ix[1]). Cenwulf, king of Mercia, to Wulfred, archbishop. (Kent)
*822	(B-370, S-55) *Cotton Augustus ii. 93* (s. ix[1]). Ceolwulf, king of Mercia and Kent, to Wulfred, archbishop. (Kent)
*823	(B-374, S-56) *Cotton Augustus ii. 75* (s. ix[1]). Ceolwulf, king of Mercia and Kent, to Wulfred, archbishop. (Kent)
*824	(B-378) *B. M. Stowe Ch. 14* (s. ix[1]). Recovery of land by Wulfred from Cwenthryth. (Kent)
*825	(B-384, S-58) *Cotton Augustus ii. 78* (s. ix[1]). Dispute between Wulfred and Cenwulf. (Middlesex and Kent)
*825	(B-384, S-58) *B. M. Stowe Ch. 15* (s. ix[1]). Dispute between Wulfred and Cenwulf.[31] (Middlesex and Kent)

---

[31] This is the last of the charters associated with Kent to be included in this study; A.D. 825 is taken as a conservative cutoff date for strong Mercian influence in Kent.

*825X832   (B-380, S-36) *Cotton Augustus ii. 72* (s. ix[1]). Wulfred,
           archbishop, to Christ Church.
*831   (B-400, S-59) *Cotton Augustus ii. 94* (s. ix[1]). Wiglaf,
           king of Mercia, to Wulfred, archbishop. (Middlesex)
836   (B-416, S-47) *Cotton Augustus ii. 9* (s. ix[1]). Wiglaf,
           king of Mercia, to the minister at Hanbury. (Worcs.)
844–845   (B-452, S-48) *Cant. DC., Chart. Ant. C. 1280* (s.
           ix med). Berthwulf, king of Mercia, to Forthred,
           his *thegn*. (Bucks.)
*873   (B-536, S-45) *B. M. Stowe Ch. 19* (s. ix[2]). Alfred,
           king of Wessex, and Æthelred, archbishop, to Liaba,
           son of Birgwine. (Kent)

The difficulties with dealing with the linguistic data of the charters
are so numerous that Anglo-Saxon scholars have all but ignored
them. Although much of the distrust of the charters can be traced
to an outmoded notion of dialect (that is, that a "pure dialect"
cannot exhibit a mixture of forms), the problems are real enough.
To begin with, the term *charter*, for a student of the language,
covers a multitude of sins: "royal grants, private agreements, wills,
records of proceedings of councils, &c."[32] Although this is an often-
repeated objection, no one has investigated the extent to which the
nature of the charter affects its language. Even if one limits oneself
to original charters or contemporary copies, problems remain.
Campbell's assessment of the problem is typical:

> Many record grants of land in Kent by West-Saxon and Mercian
> kings, and it is not possible to be sure if the extant copies reflect
> the orthographical practices of the area of the grant, or those of the
> kingdom of the monarch concerned. The reports of the proceedings
> of Church councils are not of any linguistic value, for they are invariably
> in Latin except for names, and since ecclesiastics from all parts would
> be present, the lists of their names cannot be said to represent any
> dialect at all.

[32] A. Campbell, *Old English Grammar* (Oxford: Oxford University Press,
1959), pp. 5–6.

The Sources for the Study of Early Old English

When due regard is taken to all the methods of elimination just indicated, we are left in the period before 900 with the following Mercian charters: Sweet's nos. 9, 10, 11, 12, 13, 14, 47, 48.[33]

As there have been no thorough studies of all the early charters, it is impossible to know how any of these parameters affect the language of the charters. A statement such as Campbell's is, however, amenable to empirical verification on some counts. In this study, an attempt will be made to correlate the linguistic features of the charters to the Mercian orthographic influence Kuhn observed. Thus we may determine the extent to which the extant MSS reflect the orthographic practices (by which term Campbell refers not to letter forms but to a system of phonological–orthographic correspondences) of the area of the grant or the area of the monarch concerned.

The fact that the earlier charter data are mostly limited to personal and place names written in Latin documents introduces problems of its own. As mentioned earlier, the names may be of individuals from different parts of England. It is difficult, even if one knew for sure the dialect of the scribe, to know whether the scribe would render a name according to his own pronunciation of it or would attempt to reproduce the pronunciation of the named or the local pronunciation of the places. As an added complication, the names of persons and places tend to preserve traditional spellings. To make matters worse, it is often hard to determine the extent of the Latin influence on spelling.[34]

It is premature to offer the conclusions of this study before the presentation and discussion of the data. Without strong counter-evidence, however, a safe starting point is to use the charter data as support for, but not the basis of, an understanding of the patterns of variation in the wide-ranging population of speakers of Old English. The problems of dealing with charters do not render them useless as important sources of data.

[33] Ibid., p. 6.
[34] Kuhn, "Charter Hands," p. 467.

2 Reconstituting the Sounds of Old English

The Glossaries

These three closely related MSS provide the bulk of the data that antedates the *Vespasian Psalter*.

THE EPINAL GLOSSARY, ÉPINAL BIBLIOTHÈQUE MUNICIPALE 72

It is unanimously agreed that this MS contains the most archaic linguistic forms. Sweet, in the introduction to his facsimile edition, placed the MS on paleographical grounds at the beginning of the eighth century at the latest.[35] Hessels on the basis of Thompson's early opinions argued that the MS belonged to the ninth century. Thompson, however, appears to have come around to Sweet's position. In his magnum opus, he refers to the *Epinal Glossary* as an "Anglo-Saxon glossary (8th cent.)"[36] and discusses its hand as an example of eighth-century round-hand to be associated with the hands of the *Lindisfarne Gospels*, the *Canterbury Gospels*, *Durham Cassiodorus*, early charters, etc.[37] Lowe and Ker support Sweet's claim, placing the MS in the first half of the eighth century.[38] Both also agree that the MS is distinctly Anglo-Saxon in nature. Lowe, judging by the vellum, believes it to have been written in England; Ker states that it might have been written on the Continent by an Anglo-Saxon scribe or a scribe trained at an English center. Thus, the MS can be dated with confidence in s. viii[1]. Chadwick gives abundant internal linguistic evidence for a probable dating of the language between A.D. 680 and 730.[39] The data used in this study

[35] Henry Sweet, ed., *The Epinal Glossary* (London: Trübner and Co., 1883), p. xiv.

[36] E. M. Thompson, *An Introduction to Greek and Latin Palaeography* (Oxford: Oxford University Press, 1912), p. 590.

[37] Ibid., p. 386.

[38] E. A. Lowe, ed., *Codices Latini Antiquiores* (Oxford: Oxford University Press, 1935); Neil R. Ker, *Catalogue of Manuscripts Containing Anglo-Saxon* (Oxford: Oxford University Press, 1957), p. 152.

[39] H. M. Chadwick, "Studies in Old English," *Transactions of the Cambridge Philological Society* 4 (1894–1899): 246–248.

are taken from A. Brown's edition[40] and have been collated with Sweet's and Schlutter's[41] facsimiles and with the manuscript itself.

*THE ERFURT GLOSSARY, ERFURT STADTBÜCHEREI
AMPLONIANUS F. 42*

This actually consists of three glossaries. The first is a copy deriving closely from the same archetype from which the *Epinal Glossary* descends.[42] The second and third glossaries add some 81 Old English glosses. The MS was copied by an Old High German scribe who was unfamiliar with Old English and is written in a hand typical of the script used in the Cologne cathedral school. It can be dated with certainty in the first part of the ninth century. The language, however, was fossilized by the scribe who preserves the language of his undatable exemplar. Although the language of the text and its relationship to the other texts of this study will be discussed at length in what follows, Chadwick's placement of it at circa A.D. 750 is a good starting point.[43]

*THE CORPUS GLOSSARY, CORPUS CHRISTI COLLEGE
CAMBRIDGE 144*

Contained herein are over 2000 glosses in Old English. (See Figure 2.2.) This larger collection of material had as one of its sources a descendant of the *Epinal–Erfurt* archetype. The glosses that it shares in common with the *Epinal* and *Erfurt Glossaries*, then, must be analyzed as a separate subset of the *Corpus* data. The dating of the MS has been disputed as widely as that of the *Epinal Glossary*. Hessels followed Bradshaw and Wright and thought that it must have been written in the early part of the eighth century.[44]

---

[40] A. Brown, ed., "The Epinal Glossary," Ph.D. dissertation, Stanford University, 1969.

[41] Otto B. Schlutter, ed., *Das Epinaler und Erfurter Glossar* (Hamburg: Verlag von Henri Grand, 1912).

[42] Henry Sweet, ed., *The Oldest English Texts* (Oxford: Oxford University Press, 1885), pp. 16–18.

[43] Chadwick, "Studies," pp. 248–249.

[44] John H. Hessels, ed., *An Eighth-Century Latin–Anglo-Saxon Glossary* (Cambridge: Cambridge University Press, 1890), p. ix.

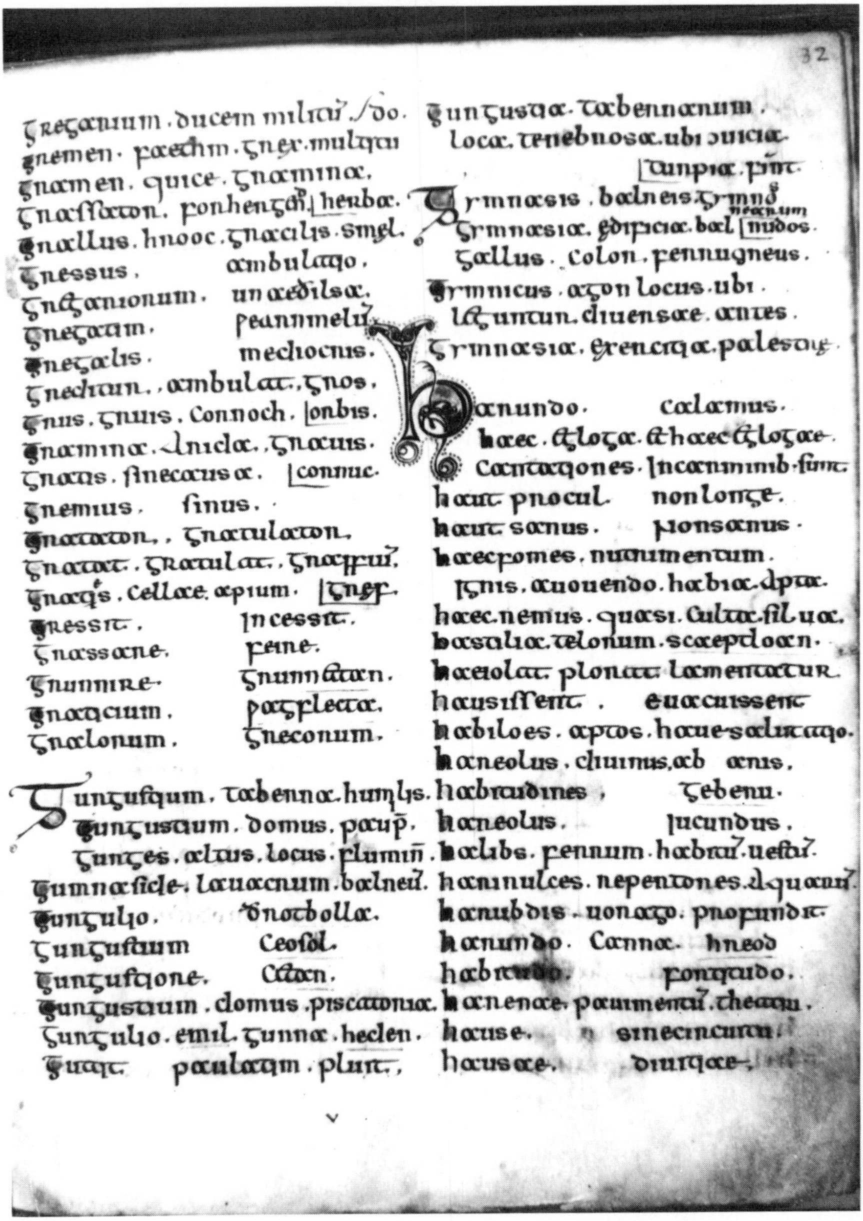

FIGURE 2.2. *The Corpus Glossary.* (Corpus Christi College, Cambridge 144, by permission of the Master and Fellows of Corpus Christi College.)

Orchi. testiculi.
Oratones. spelbodan.
Oraculū. responsū diuini.
Onbamin. onbanoe. Gū.
Ona. natione. fines.
Onsa. inchoate.
Onsus. locutus. ona. frons.
Ondo. equesten. equitum, ondo.
Onnus. genus. ligni.
Onbatus. apffb; destructu
Onigenania. uennacu
Onaton. facundus.
Ondinatus. gehæplice.
On. ongimendi.
Onpleut. conpleut.
Onion. ebundnung. tun.
Onaculum. ubisondes. auqun
Onbus. qui filios. ñ abet/ļi.
Onigenani. uennacu
Oneoe. frenoe.
Ongea. mistenia. bacchi.
ondo. equesten. pnosenatum.
Onoma. uisus. nomæne.
Onbia. sifan. utunda.
Onbita. strnata. / nacuī.
Onto. gnafia. discnipto. litte
Ondinanius. milis. qui Jntegno.
ondine. militat.
Onbitoe. laeft.

Oscillae. totnidan.
Ostuim. punpune.
Oscines. auspicia.

Osci os. apeni. hoc est.
Oscitantes. geongendi.
Ostentin. ostentio.
Ofdum. ab obstando. dicimi.
Osee. saluaton. Of mae. since.
Osanna. odñe saluifica. po
    pulum. tuū. ostanata. despenat
Ostrigen. bnuunbeosu.
Ossan. nñ mont. oqui. quies.
Osga. extins. fluminum. jnm..
Oscatann. Cnaes maun
Ostentim. monstrum
Osinus. odrtunus.
Ostentat. multo. offendit
Ostentane. demos finane.
Osanna. genus. ligni.

Othus. semen mundi.
Oqum. qui es. secunitas.
uaccuatus. oqosus. quietus.

Ouantes. gaudentes.

Oz-asanga militū. caelcia
    menta. Ozias. fongtaido. dñ

Paltnionchae. pnini. panu.
    panimomū. gestnion.
Panima. scutum.
Panam. sumedaeli.
Palpntans. bnogdstende
Pantriculatam. st rccimelum
Paludamentum. genus. uestî
menn bellici. hæcile.

Sweet was more conservative and maintained that the handwriting was "not latter than the first half of the eighth century."[45] Chadwick pointed out that while the MS was dated before or contemporary with the *Epinal Glossary*, the linguistic forms point to the end of the eighth or beginning of the ninth century.[46] Modern paleographers substantiate the date that Chadwick inferred from linguistic considerations; Lowe and Ker agree in placing the MS at the turn of the ninth century.[47] The data, taken from Lindsay's edition, were collated with a microfilm of the MS and the MS itself.

THE LEIDEN GLOSSARY, RIJKSUNIVERSITEIT VOSSIANUS LAT. 4° 69

Some 259 Anglo-Saxon words are added to our corpus of data. Its compiler obviously drew from some of the sources common to the compilers of the *Epinal–Erfurt* archetype and the *Corpus* archetype. The two scribes who copied the MS wrote in a hand that can be linked closely to the scripts employed at St. Gallen in numerous MSS dating A.D. 754–800. The scribes were apparently ignorant of Old English; the glosses indicate a marked Old German influence. The data were taken from Hessels's edition and were collated against a microfilm of the MS.

THE GLOSSARIES AS DATA

The major difficulties encountered in the analysis of the data from the glossaries are related to the manner in which the texts were assembled. In order to insure that the church fathers could continue to be read and understood, monks made lists (for individual texts) of difficult Latin words and glossed them with more familiar Latin words. In that manner, sets of glosses were collected to such works as those of Aldhelm's *De Laude Virginitatis*, Jerome's *De Viris Illustribus*, Isidore of Seville's *De Summo Bono*, Gregory's *Dialogues*, etc. Monasteries wanting to develop as complete a corpus

---

[45] Sweet, *Texts*, p. 5.
[46] Chadwick, "Studies," p. 249.
[47] Lowe, *Codices*, p. 3; Ker, *Catalogue*, p. 49.

as possible would pool their resources. More general glossaries were then formed by rudely alphabetizing the glosses from several sources. As the vernacular languages became more important in monastic life and as the knowledge of Latin deteriorated, Germanic words would find their way into the glossaries. The problem arises in that it is impossible to know when and where an Old English gloss entered the corpus. In addition, scribes sporadically modernized (according to their own inclinations) glosses they were copying. As none of the glossaries is an original, we do not know, for example, how many redactions lie between either the *Epinal* or *Erfurt Glossaries* and their common original, nor how long the forms in the archetype would continue to be an influence on subsequent copies. Chadwick has done an admirable job with the difficult task of reconstructing the probable forms of the *Epinal–Erfurt* archetype. Using his work and our knowledge of early forms and their later developments, it is possible to assess which sound changes must have been synchronic in the dialect of the copyist.

Bede's *History*

The *British Museum Cotton Tiberius C. ii* (s. viii) is one of the four oldest surviving copies of Bede's *Historia Ecclesiastica*. It is of special interest to this investigation because it was produced in a Mercian center.[48] While the names in the other three early Bede MSS show Northumbrian forms, the scribe of the *Cotton Tiberius C. II* has consistently rendered the names in Mercian form. The names, consequently, provide a very early source of data. In addition to the names, a total of 89 glosses and their Latin *lemmata* were added to the ends of books of the *History*. Paleographers assign the hand of these glosses to the late ninth or early tenth century.

Throughout the folios of the Latin text, several scribes have scratched Old English interpretations over difficult Latin words.

[48] Sherman M. Kuhn, "From Canterbury to Lichfield," *Speculum* 23 (1948): 613–619.

The hands are difficult to separate and cannot, as yet, be dated with accuracy, although Meritt thinks them tenth century at the latest.[49] Many of the glosses are extremely difficult to read and were missed by Meritt who used only direct sunlight in his attempts to read them. I have undertaken reading the glosses missed by Meritt and have attempted to distinguish between the hands of the annotators.

The *Blickling Psalter*

Pierpont Morgan Library MS. 776 contains an eighth-century Roman version of the Psalms. The manuscript ornamentation points to a non-Northumbrian origin; its illuminations are very closely related to those of the Mercian Bede, the *Book of Cerne*, the *Codex Aureus*, and the *Vespasian Psalter*. There are, in fact, so many similarities between its initials and the initials of the *Vespasian Psalter* that it is hard to imagine that they are not the work of the same illuminator. Twenty-one glosses, "written in the same red ink as that used for the rubrics,"[50] are scattered throughout the manuscript. Ker has assigned them to the ninth century,[51] but they are almost certainly contemporary with the manuscript. Numerous later glosses are not of interest to this study.

The *Book of Cerne*

Cambridge University Library MS. Ll. 1. 10 contains a richly illuminated prayer book known as the *Book of Cerne*. Since the manuscript twice includes the name Ædelwald, the bishop of Lichfield from A.D. 818 to 830, it can be dated and localized with precision.[52]

---

[49] H. D. Meritt, *Old English Glosses* (New York: The Modern Language Association of America, 1945), p. 4.

[50] Sweet, *Texts*, p. 122.

[51] Ker, *Catalogue*, p. 348.

[52] Kuhn, "Lichfield," pp. 619–627, although David Dumville has argued

Old English has been added to the text in two places. The book begins with an incomplete prayer written on a previously blank page. The prayer, usually referred to as the *Lorica Prayer*, is written in a hand very similar to that of the body of the text. It contains Mercian letter forms also found in the Latin text.

THE LORICA OF GILDAS

Contained in the *Book of Cerne*, this includes 74 Old English glosses written in a hand contemporary with the manuscript (if not the hand of the text). The glossing was completed by a tenth-century scribe. These later glosses are not relevant to this work.

The *Vespasian Psalter*

The questions of the precise dating and provenience of the *B. M. Cotton Vespasian A. 1* have inspired one of the hottest controversies in Anglo-Saxon studies.[53] In the absence of conclusive internal evidence, such questions cannot be resolved with certainty. Suffice it to say that Sherman M. Kuhn has amassed evidence to establish a reasonable probability of its Mercian origin.[54] Although Kuhn would have the *Psalter* and its related texts all produced in the neighborhood of Lichfield, such precise location of provenience is probably neither possible nor necessary. No one doubts that the manuscript was produced at a time when Mercian kings were supreme; early Mercian influence is well attested at Canterbury. Since Mercian kings made bishops and controlled the granting of land and other

---

convincingly that the *Book of Cerne* is a copy of a Northumbrian manuscript ("Liturgical Drama and Panegyric Responsory from the Eighth Century: A Re-examination of the Origin and Contents of the Ninth-Century Section of the Book of Cerne," *The Journal of Theological Studies, New Series,* 23.2 (1972): 374–406).

[53] See Minnie Cate Morrell, *A Manual of Old English Biblical Materials* (Knoxville: The University of Tennessee Press, 1965), pp. 72–81 for a cogent summary of the arguments.

[54] Kuhn, "Lichfield."

privileges, there must have been constant intercourse between Canterbury and Lichfield which no doubt included exchange of scribes, illuminators, and books as well as bishops. But even if Canterbury origin be granted for the *Psalter,* its interlinear gloss is quite a different matter. (See Figure 2.3.) Kuhn has well documented the Mercian orthographic influence in the gloss.[55] Further, the gloss exhibits a regular phonological system which is non-Northumbrian, non-West Saxon, and non-Kentish. In addition, the early Middle English texts of the West Midlands possess phonological features that are developments of the language of the *Psalter.* No matter where the gloss was produced, it is certainly Mercian of the first part of the ninth century.

The *Minora*

THE CODEX AUREUS INSCRIPTION

An inscription recording the gift of the *Codex Aureus* (now in the Kungl. Bibliotek in Stockholm) to Christ Church is found on folio 11 of the manuscript. The grantor, Ælfred *aldormon,* has been identified as an earl of Surrey who died in A.D. 871. Thus, the Old English of the inscription can be localized in Surrey and dated between A.D. 853 (when Ælfred became earl) and 871.

THE ROYAL GLOSSES

B. M. Royal 2.a.xx is an Anglo-Saxon prayer book assigned to the first half of the eighth century. Several prayers are interlinearly glossed in Old English. Ker assigns the hand to the first half of the tenth century.[56] Zupitza's edition, which I have checked against the manuscript, has been used for this study.

THE MARTYROLOGY FRAGMENTS

Two late ninth-century fragments of the Old English *Martyrology* are preserved in *B. M. Additional MSS 23211* and *40165B.* The

---

[55] Kuhn, "Charter Hands."
[56] Ker, *Catalogue,* p. 456.

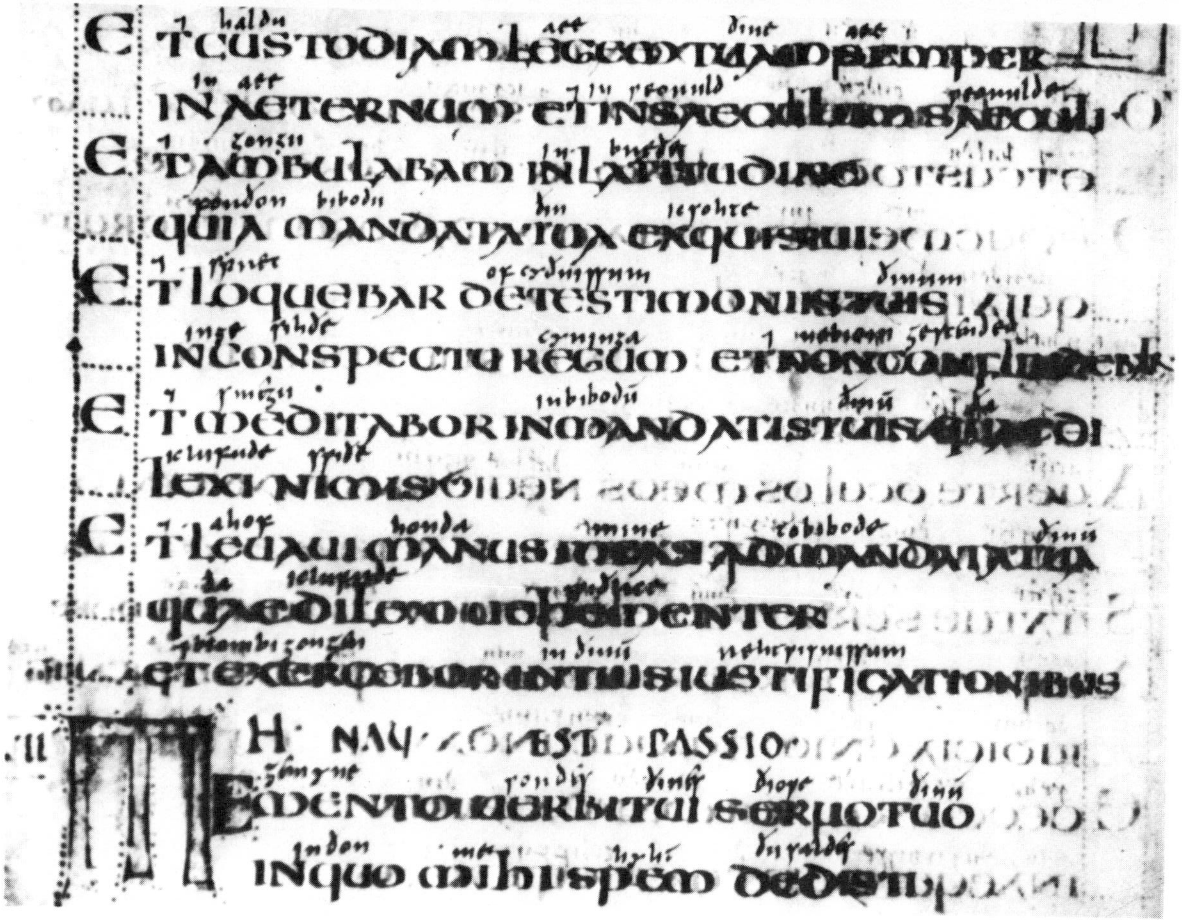

FIGURE 2.3. *The Vespasian Psalter.* (British Museum Cotton Vespasian A.1, by permission of the British library.)

former was edited by Sweet, the latter by Celia Sisam.[57] Both texts are West Saxon copies of Mercian originals.

THE OMONT LEAF

Probably the most interesting and important of the minor Old English texts is a recently discovered fragment, *Louvain, Bibliothèque Centrale de l'Université, Section des manuscrits, Fragmenta H. Omont no. 3*.[58] Nothing is known of the manuscript's origin; it was discovered as part of the Louvain collection of the personal library of M. Henri Omont. The fragment is a full folio leaf, measuring 20.7 × 15.5 cm. Pen practices and alphabets on the verso exhibit orthographic features that suggest that the leaf was prepared for writing (and used for scribbling) in a continental center in the seventh or eighth century. The text of the recto contains medical/semimagical recipes for treatment of swellings and other ills. It is extremely difficult to date and localize a fragment that cannot be recognized as a missing portion of a well-identified manuscript. Further, the text is unique enough in its orthography and language to present a tantalizing puzzle. The handwriting of the recto is clearly insular in character and is conservative in letter forms. Old English [æ], for example, is written *ae*, or *e-caudata*, but never *æ* (see page 48). Although the state of the unstressed vowels would argue for a later date, the stressed vowels so exactly match those of the *Corpus Glossary* that it is hard not to conclude that the leaf is a close contemporary of that text. The two texts share some 43 vocabulary items that are identical except for minor orthographic variants:[59]

[57] Celia Sisam, "An Early Fragment of the *Old English Martyrology*," *Review of English Studies*, New Series iv (1953): 209–220.

[58] The *Omont Leaf* is catalogued by Neil R. Ker, "A Supplement to *The Catalogue of Manuscripts Containing Anglo-Saxon*," *Anglo-Saxon England* 5 (1976), p. 128; it is printed and described by Bella Schauman and Angus Cameron, "A Newly-found Leaf of Old English from Louvain," *Anglia: Zeitschrift für Englische Philologie* 95 (1977), pp. 289–312.

[59] Schauman and Cameron, "Newly-found Leaf," pp. 310–311.

The Sources for the Study of Early Old English

Omont Leaf	Corpus Glossary
aac	*aac*
aec (2x)	*aec*
aesc	*aesc*
ęscðrote	*aescðrote*
asuoln	*asuollen*
beolonan	*belone*
biað	*biað*
biscopw(yrt	*biscopuuyrt*
bollan	*bolla*
cinen	*cinendi*
clęn	*claemende*
cnio	*cnio*
cuiicbean	*cuicbeam*
drenc	*-drenc*
eofordrote	*eoforþrote*
eolone	*eolone*
felle	*fel*
gemęng	*gemaengan*
gyrdels	*gyrdels*
hręfnesfot	*hraefnesfoot*
hwitcudu	*huitcudu*
ifign	*ifegn*
mið (2X)	*mið*
nęhterne	*naeht-*
neodowarde	*neoþouard*
netlan	*netlan*
ribbe	*ribbe*
salf	*salf*
scęden(ne	*scaed*
scoas	*scoh*
seech	*secg*
slahðorn	*slahðorn*
suę	*suae*
suefl	*suefl-*
ðeh (3X)	*thegh*
walwyrt	*walhwyrt*

The *Omont Leaf*, then, can be assigned with reasonable assurance to the ninth century. Schauman and Cameron "would date it between A.D. 850 and 900, and place it at a scriptorium where Mercian conventions of writing were observed."[60] That would make the *Omont Leaf* the oldest nondocumentary, nonreligious piece of Old English prose—a very important text.

THE TEXTS IN CONTEXT

The foregoing summary of facts about the earliest English texts fails to account for them in one critically important way: These texts are art historical monuments of exquisite beauty. Although they were written at a time when book production was costly indeed, we unfailingly find the best of materials, wide margins, spacious (and uneconomical) hands, and (as in the case of the reproduction from the *Corpus Glossary*) illuminated capitals of subtle and intricate design. The presence of English glosses in these texts indicates that the addition of the vernacular was considered a further adornment to these deluxe productions—powerful testimony of the privileged position of the written (English) word in Anglo-Saxon culture. Such books could only be produced at times of plenty and relative social and political stability. They were most likely produced at centers enjoying royal patronage, where, of course, political influences would be most strongly felt. These books may even have been produced at royal command or as presentation copies to royal persons. After all, a psalter is a quintessentially royal book; the songs of a king make a fitting prayer book for a king. In the *Vespasian Psalter* painting of King David playing his conspicuously Anglo-Saxon harp, we may be invited to see the type of a perfect Anglo-Saxon king. A late ninth-century charter specifies the way in which royal patrons are to be remembered:

[60] Ibid., p. 312.

> At every matins and at every vespers and at every tierce, the *De profundis* as long as they live, and after their death *Laudate Dominum;* and every Saturday in St. Peter's church thirty psalms and a Mass for them. . . .[61]

A deluxe psalter would be an appropriate production for such a community as received this change. We have already observed how fitting a gift a copy of Bede's *History* would be for a Mercian king, both because of its admonitions on Christian kingship and its testimony of Mercian supremacy. The Mercian Bede (copied in the time of Æðelbald and Offa), unlike other contemporary Bede texts, is a highly decorated volume. We know that King Offa possessed his own Bede, and we might wonder if the *Cotton Tiberius C ii* was made for him. At any rate, the nature and style of these first English manuscripts reinforce our sense of the interrelatedness of literacy and the coalition of church and state.

Figure 2.4 diagrams the historical, political, social, and intellectual context within which the Mercian Old English texts appeared. The construction of the *Tribal Hidage* was among the first Mercian acts of literacy. The text formalized the economic base for the Mercian hegemony. The revenue derived from the *Hidage* made possible the construction of Mercian defensive dykes along the western frontier; the ability to assess taxes no doubt encouraged the production of coins and the regulation of their integrity. The resultant political stability enabled the solidification of the powers of the Mercian kings, and charters were drawn up to define and confirm royal prerogatives. Royal support for the major religious houses made possible the extensive production of fine manuscripts. The expansion of libraries reinforced the Mercian renaissance of Latin learning. As literacy flourished in the Roman mode, attention was directed to the writing of genealogies and the codification of laws. With the establishment of a royal scriptorium, peculiarly Mercian orthographic practices developed and the production of charters mushroomed.

[61] Dorothy Whitelock, *English Historical Documents c. 500–1042* (London: Eyre & Spottiswoode, 1955), p. 598.

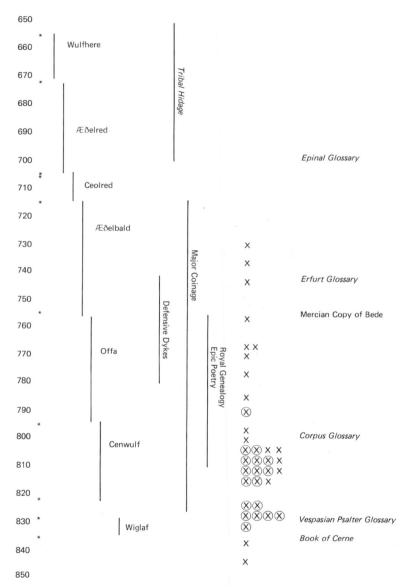

FIGURE 2.4. The products of literacy in their political context. (×s are individual charters; ⊗s are charters that contain Mercian letter forms.)

86

(Notice the dramatic hiatus in charters which resulted from the quarrel between Cenwulf and the archbishop of Canterbury.) From the same period in which all charters exhibit Mercian letter forms, we find the *Vespasian Psalter* gloss, also with its Mercian letter forms. The writing of the most thoroughly Mercian text coincides with the apex of Mercian influence on literacy. The consolidation of Anglo-Saxon politics and culture was the development of *English* politics and culture largely because of the act of *English* kings writing in the *English* language.

3

POLITICS AND LANGUAGE CHANGE

NE of the most striking differences between the language of the earliest and latest texts of the Mercian period is the way in which the early Old English *a* that developed from West Germanic **a* was spelled when it occurred before nasal consonants. The usual development of West Germanic **a* was a fronting to [æ], but the fronting was retarded when the sound was found in syllables closed with a nasal consonant or in syllables that preceded another syllable containing a back vowel. The effect of this prehistoric change on Old English allophonic alternations has been discussed on page 51. The resulting nasalized vowel was always written with an *o* in the *Vespasian Psalter;* it was written with an *a* in the *Epinal Glossary,* the earliest text of this study. Spellings fluctuate between *a* and *o* in the texts of the intervening period of Mercian political control of southern England. It is typical of previous studies of Old English that the variation in the spelling of the nasalized vowel was noted, then promptly dismissed as free variation or scribal uncertainty due to "dialect mixture." Upon closer scrutiny we discover not "free" variation, but variation patterned and constrained by phonetic environment. One would expect that the variation generated by scribal uncertainty would be perfectly random, patterned only occasionally by chance. Before presenting the data for the development of nasalized early Old English *a* in the texts that are the special concern of this study, it will be helpful to sketch the general history of this sound change in the other attested varieties of early Old English.

90

THE CHANGE IN OLD NORTHUMBRIAN

There are scant data which give evidence of the early Northumbrian development of West Germanic *a before nasals. Early eighth-century Northumbrian texts (the Latin manuscripts of Bede's *History*, *Cædmon's Hymn*, the Franks Casket, and *Bede's Death Song*) already exhibit evidence for the development to a sound represented by *o* (probably [ɔ]). The personal names in Bede[1] are almost evenly split between *a* and *o*, even though many of the persons named are southerners who probably spelled their names with an *a*. The remaining sources are, of course, too brief to be conclusive, but it is worth observing the predominance of the *o* spelling: the Frank's Casket (*hronæs, giswom*), *Cædmon's Hymn* (*modgidanc, moncynnæs, Cædmon*), *Bede's Death Song* (*thoncsnotturra, than, hiniong[a]e*). There is an unfortunate gap between these tests and the tenth-century *Lindisfarne Gospels, Durham Ritual,* and *Rushworth II*. Scant data for the intervening period are available from names in the *Liber Vitae Dunelmensis* where *o* is the rule (the early Northumbrian king *Anna*, the exception). The tenth-century Northumbrian texts have *o* nearly universally except in the singular of the past tense of Class Three strong verbs.[2] The poem called *Durham*[3] offers a final glimpse at the development in Northumbrian Old English; internal evidence allows for accurate dating of the composition of the poem between A.D. 1104 and 1109.[4] The surviving MS, *Cambridge University Library Ff. 1. 27,* was written in the late part of the twelfth century. A second MS of the poem was destroyed in the Cottonian Library fire, but fortunately Hickes printed a transcript of the burned *B. M. Cotton Vitellius D. xx,* dated by Wanley s. xiii[in]. Since the poet has intimate knowledge of Durham, Nor-

[1] Hilmer Ström, *Old English Personal Names in Bede's History* (Lund: Hakan Ohlsson, 1939), p. 101.

[2] A. Campbell, *Old English Grammar* (Oxford: Oxford University Press, 1959), p. 51.

[3] Elliott Van Kirk Dobbie, *The Anglo-Saxon Minor Poems* (New York: Columbia University Press, 1942), p. 27.

[4] Ibid., pp. xliv–xlv.

thumbrian saints, etc., we assume he was probably a Northumbrian. The language of the texts supports this assumption. Several Anglian features are to be noted: *ch* spellings, false gemination in *steppu*, and confusion of *ea* and *eo*. The *-ern* of *fæstern* and *ðe* as the definite article are strong, specifically Northumbrian indicators. In addition, *gecheðe* (Cambridge MS) and *gichedðe* (Cotton MS) are corruptions of Lindisfarne *gigoð*. The poem's four instances of WGmc. **a* before nasals are spelled with *o: gemonge, monige, monia, genom*.

THE DEVELOPMENT IN EARLY WEST SAXON

The MSS (Parker *Chronicle*, Ælfred's translations of the *Cura Pastoralis* and *Orosius*) from which our knowledge of early West Saxon derives exhibit fluctuation in the representation of this sound. Cosijn, while stating that there is no hard and fast rule, agrees with Sweet that

> nur wörter, die selten oder nie den ton haben, zeigen durchweg oder stets *o;* im allgemeinen scheinen weniger gebrauchte wörter das *a* an bevorzugen, häufiger gebrauchte das *o*.[5]

For example, the *Cura* MSS have *a:o* in a ratio of 3:4, the *Orosius*, 1:3. Cosijn's speculation and the following observation by Miller suggest that these data themselves would be an interesting subject for a study of lexical diffusion:

> *Mon* and its kindred enter in largely. Indeed in all documents everywhere *mon* enters in early, and is among the latest to retire.[6]

In late West Saxon tests, *a* spellings are the rule. The discrepancy between early West Saxon variation and late West Saxon *a* becomes

[5] Peter Jakob Cosijn, *Altwestsächsische Grammatik* (Haag: Martinus Nijhoff, 1888), p. 13.
[6] Thomas Miller, *Place Names in the English Bede* (Strassburg: Karl J. Trübner, 1896), p. 9.

less mysterious when we realize that the scribes of Ælfred's manuscripts were only one (at most two) generations away from scriptoria run by Mercians who regularly spelled the sound with an *o*.

THE DATA FROM OLD KENTISH

A glance at the Kentish charters is instructive. Consider the following four charters which antedate the period of Mercian control:

Date	Charter	Number of *a* forms	Number of *o* forms
679[7]	*Aug. ii 2*	1	0
700	*Aug. ii 88*	1	0
732	*Aug. ii 91*	2	0
741	*Aug. ii 101*	1	0

The data are scant but unanimous in *a* forms. The word *Cantuariorum* accounts for four of the occurrences of WGmc. **a*. As further testimony to the native spelling of the sound in this word, it is to be noted that the people of Kent are regularly, even in Mercian charters, called *cantuariorum*, only once *contuariorum*. There is a dramatic change in the charters produced under Mercian domination. The manuscripts almost exclusively have *o* spellings (64 times) with *a* occurring only in *cantuariorum* and *cantuarabyrg*. In the following listing, charters marked with an asterisk were found by Kuhn to evidence Mercian orthographic influence.

Date	Charter	Number of *a* forms	Number of *o* forms
803	*Cant. C. 1*	0	3
*805	*Stowe 8*	0	12
*805X810	*Aug. ii. 79*	0	34
*811	*Aug. ii 47*	0	11
*825X832	*Aug. ii 72*	0	2
*824	*Stowe 14*	0	2

[7] Although this document survives only in an early eighth-century copy, the copy preserves archaic spellings.

3 Politics and Language Change

The following four charters, only two of which contain Mercian letter forms, represent the state of the language during the first years after the beginning of the decay of Mercian influence:

Date	Charter	Number of *a* forms	Number of *o* forms
*833X839	*Aug. ii 64*	11	40
845X853	*Aug. ii 42*	0	13
850	*Aug. ii 52*	10	4
*867X870	*Aug. ii 19*	2	8

Since the transition was not cataclysmic, these data are what one would expect. Mercian religious would continue to live in Kent, and native Kentish scribes trained under Mercian domination would continue to exert an influence for about one generation (until c. 850). Spellings vary between *a* and *o*, but *o* is the more common especially in the earlier charters and the charter containing Mercian letter forms.

The British Museum Charter *Aug. ii 92* (B-405) is especially instructive for the state of the language during the transitional period. It contains two parts: an initial grant to Christ Church by Lufu (now dated by scholars at A.D. 843) and an addition in the same hand but by a different scribe (not later than A.D. 863). There are clear examples of Mercian *t* and *g* in the first part. The nasal *a* is there spelled *o* twice, *a* once. The second part of the document has no Mercian letter forms and only *a* spellings (six times).

Four charters give data for the second generation after the beginning of the Mercian exodus.

Date	Charter	Number of *a* forms	Number of *o* forms
859	*Aug. ii 16*	4	1 K^2
863	*Cant. M 14*	2	1
863X867	*Stowe 16*	6	1
868	*Aug. ii 17*	1	0 K^2

The *a* spellings predominate (15:3); only corrupt or compromise Mercian letter forms (here marked as K^2) are to be found.

The Data from Old Kentish

The late Kentish charters exhibit only *a* for the nasal *a* in fully stressed words; *o* appears regularly in weakly stressed words as in the early West Saxon texts of the period.

Date	Charter	Number of *a* forms	Number of *o* forms
958	*Stowe 26*	7	0
988	*Cott. Ch. viii 20*	5	0
1038	*Aug. ii 90*	6	0
1044	*Aug. ii 35*	3	0
1044	*Aug. ii 70*	4	0

The data taken as a whole point either to Mercian influence or to an independent (but temporary) Kentish development of [a] to [ɔ]. If the change was independent, its rise and decline is curiously concomitant with Mercian supremacy. At any rate, the data cannot be dismissed as sporadic variation between *a* and *o*.

The interlinear gloss to the *B. M. Cotton Vespasian D. vi*, the so-called *Kentish Glosses*, contains 27 words that have a vowel developed from WGmc. **a* before nasals:[8]

mon (4X)	*hand*
strongeste	*strangere*
þonne (9X)	*unstran*
hwonon	*gestrangad(e* (4X)
fromiað	*geðancum*
	ðanne
	stran
	biðafandan
	afododlic
	na(m
	wam
	bioðgesa(m
	fra(m (4X)

[8] These data are taken from Irene Williams, "A Grammatical Investigation of the Old Kentish Glosses," *Bonner Beiträge zur Anglistik* Vol. 19 (Bonn: P. Haustein's Verlag, 1905).

forspanegu(m
forspanen
wana
lamp
biðgewaned
scanan
manegn (2X)
angað
þane

The analysis of these data is complicated by a couple of factors. First, the gloss shows a marked West Saxon influence whose effect on the language of the gloss with respect to this sound change is difficult to assess. Second, while the date of the MS is fairly clear (s. xi med.), the text is probably a copy of an earlier, already glossed MS—two hymns are spaced for a gloss which was never entered. The date and provenience of the exemplar are not known. What can be said is that this text with notable Kentish features evidences a fluctuation between *a* and *o* (65% *a*) that parallels the Kentish-Mercian charters discussed earlier. Note that the words that occur more than once are remarkably consistent in the shape of their vowel: *mon* (4X), *þonne* (9X), *gestrangad(e* (4X), *fra(m* (4X), *manegn* (2X). Data of this sort, especially with the fossil *mon*, strongly suggest that the language is changing one word at a time. If one excludes the occurrences of *mon* and *þonne* (often weakly stressed), the ratio of *a:o* graphs becomes 29:3 (90% *a*).

DIFFUSION THROUGH THE MERCIAN
SPEECH COMMUNITY

These data attest an early Old English sound change which began in the north and diffused with varying tenacity into the rest of England during the period of Mercian supremacy. The politically motivated process was reversed by the fact of West Saxon domination

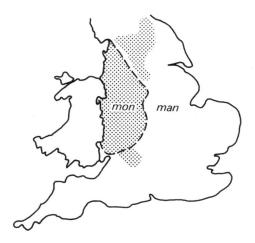

FIGURE 3.1. The Middle English *mon/man* isogloss.

toward the end of the Old English period, except in the Mercian homeland West Midlands where *o* spellings are found throughout the Middle English period. In view of the permanence of *mon*, Figure 3.1 is of particular interest. The shaded areas in the map represent Wright's observation of a modern [ɔ] in *man*.[9] Moore, Meech, and Whitehall's fifteenth-century *mon/man* isogloss is marked by a broken line.[10] (See Figure 3.1.) That the seeds of this development can be seen in the structured variation of the *o* and *a* graphs of Mercian texts is an important thesis of this study. The balance of this chapter is devoted to a detailed analysis of the patterns of that variation.

[9] Joseph Wright, *The English Dialect Grammar* (Oxford: Oxford University Press, 1968), p. 26.
[10] Samuel Moore, Sanford B. Meech, and Harold Whitehall, "Middle English Dialect Characteristics and Dialect Boundaries," *Essays and Studies in English and Comparative Literature* Vol. 13 (Ann Arbor: University of Michigan Press, 1935), Insert Map.

3 Politics and Language Change

DATA FROM THE GLOSSARIES

The early eighth-century *Epinal Glossary*, whose language may reflect an even earlier period (c. A.D. 700), has *a* consistently as the development of WGmc. **a* before nasals. In only one case, *onættae*, out of 59 examples, is there an *o*. The names from the Mercian manuscript of Bede's *History* reflect the state of the language c. A.D. 735. Those named who have non-Northumbrian connections are predominantly spelled with *a* (*Tondberct*, Prince of the south Gyrwe, is the exception): *Anna*, King of the East Angles (seven times); *Iaruman*, Bishop of Mercia (four times); *Andhun*, Prince of the South Saxon (once). The names of the Northumbrians are spelled with an *o: Tilmon*, Monk (once); *Tondheri*, thegn of Oswini (once). Unfortunately, there are no data from coins, and the first relevant forms occur in the charters for A.D. 736 and 759. The *Epinal Glossary* does, however, provide a terminus a quo for the change from *a* to *o* before nasal consonants.

The language of the *Erfurt Glossary* shows considerable development from that of the *Epinal Glossary* (and hence presumably from that of their common archetype). Looking at the data as a whole, the *a:o* ratio is 32:33.

/__m	
a	*o*
ambras	*ompre*
-camb	*ombar*
haam	*from*
hama	*hom*
camb	*scom*
ambaet	*fromlicae*
hramsa	*hromsa* (*o* written over *a*)
saum	
fram	
ambechtae	

Data from the Glossaries

/—n

a	o
ansuand	brondrad
granæ	mondi
mand	onmod
landae	uuonan
anseot	hondgong
handmitta	-ponne
candelthuist	on
anhæbd	hond
an-	hron
ganot	rond
uuannan	sondae
handful	-hona
suan	onhrisit
andleac	gespon
breitibannæ	-don
assuant	brond
anstigan	uuond
stanc	uuondæ
an	huuonan
	scoritmon
	monung
	ordoncum
	ond

/—ŋ

a	o
anga	hondgong
angreta	bigongum
	gimong

To these data may be added examples from Erfurt's second glossary (*hramsa, gandi*) and third glossary (*stam, randberg, mond, manu*). Since all three Erfurt glossaries were copied by the same scribe, one might question why the data from the second and third glossaries are kept separate. It has been previously noted that the copyist of the *Erfurt Glossaries* was himself ignorant of Old English. He consistently makes errors that could not be made by a speaker of Old English. Consequently, it is not his dialect but the dialect of his exemplar that is of interest here. There is no reason to assume that all three glossaries derive from the same source. These data, in fact, argue against such an assumption. The second and third glossaries depart significantly from the first with regard to WGmc. *a* before nasal consonants: the ratio of *a:o* is 2:0 for the second, 3:1 for the third.

The overall distribution of 50% *o* is an unnecessary misrepresentation of the data:

	/__m	/__n	/__ŋ
a	10	20	2
o	7	23	3

In fact, a further breakdown of the data reveals that the divergence is due to the phonetic environment of [m] plus homorganic consonant:

	/__m-	/__mC$_h$	/__n-	/__nC$_h$
a	5	5	12	8
o	5	2	15	8

The data can be restated as a variable rule.

$$a \rightarrow \langle o \rangle \; / \_ \begin{array}{ll} n & .55 \\ \eta & .60 \\ nC_h & .50 \\ m & .50 \\ mC_h & .30 \end{array}$$

The *Leyden Glossary* shows variation (*a:o* = 5:11), but there is insufficient material to establish patterns.

/__m

a	o
hamme	homme
	ompre

/__n

a	o
and	monung
ordancas	gronae
gespan	onga
	hona
	hron
	nord (for rond)
	hond
	brond
	uoond

Viewed in relationship with the glossaries which also derive from the common archetype, the *Corpus* data are very interesting. Their analysis should begin with a consideration of the glosses common to *Epinal* and *Erfurt* (derived from their shared source):

/__m

a	o
ambras	hromsa
-camb	hromsan
ha[a]m	suom
hama	from
camb	hom
ambaect	scomo
ampre	fromlice
amber	omer

/__n

a	o
asuand	holthona
granae	on-

3 Politics and Language Change

/__n

a	*o*
mand	*gonot*
-lande	*wonnan*
ansceat	*hondful*
andmita	*suon*
candeltuist	*oncqseta*
mand	*onlaec*
brandrad	*ponne*
mand	*asuond*
anmood	*stonc*
wanan	*on-*
hand-	*-ponne*
	on-
	hond
	hon (for *hron*)
	rond
	sondȩ
	hona
	onga
	onhrioseð
	gespon
	-ðon
	brond
	wond
	wonde
	huonan
	wlonce
	-ponne
	onsueop
	onligenre
	onsuebdum

/__ŋ

a	*o*
bigangum	*gimong*
-gand (for *gang*)	

102

Data from the Glossaries

The *a/o* occurrences are summarized as follows:

	/__m	/__n	/__ŋ	/__mC$_h$	/__nC$_h$
a	2	4	2	6	9
o	8	24	1	0	8

These data attest a development of the trends noted in the *Erfurt Glossary*. Note that before [m] plus a homorganic consonant, *a* is the only form found in all six instances. Conversely, *o* is four times as frequent as *a* elsewhere before [m]. Homorganic clusters with *n* have a less prominent, yet discernible, hindering effect. The vowel is written *o* 43% of the time before such clusters, as opposed to 85% of the time elsewhere before *n*.

The effect of the *Epinal–Erfurt* archetype can be made clear by comparison of the above tendencies with those found in the glosses not derived from the common source.

/__ŋ

a	*o*
gegangendo	gecrong
gegandende	aeggimong
aegmang	tong
	ongong (2X)

/__m

a	*o*
ampre	fromlice (3X)
	fromra
	lomb
	omber
	monna (for monra)
	hom
	wom
	from
	stom (2X)
	feðrhoman

3 Politics and Language Change

$$/\_\_n$$

a	o
mand (2X)	*orðonc*
handle	*-ponne*
andwisnis	*hond* (2X)
ansuaep	*brond*
anfindo	*asuond*
suan (2X)	*horn* (with metathesis)
hran	*gabulrond*
anoða	*condel* (2X)
þanan	*blondu*
	geblonded
	huonhlot
	scond
	lond
	ond
	on-
	insondgewearp
	onhlingo
	onheawas
	onsaelid
	onginnendi
	cornuc
	onseacan
	onfilti
	onsuapen
	eorodmon
	fon
	hona
	wonung
	seofbonan
	geabulesmonung
	windfona
	cornoch

Considering that the *Corpus* scribe was copying from lists compiled earlier even in the case of the noncommon glosses, one concludes that the sound change, if not complete, is rapidly approaching completion. The *Corpus* noncommon data summarized are:

Data from the Glossaries

	/__m	/__n	/__ŋ	/__mC_h	/__nC_h
a	0	7	3	1	4
o	13	21	6	2	11

But for one gloss, the change to *o* before [m] would be complete. The constraining effect of homogranic clusters has declined. Of particular interest is the consistency with which individual lexical items are treated. Eight words occur two or more times: *gegangend* (2X), *ongong* (2X), *fromlice* (3X), *stom* (2X), *hond* (2X), *condel* (2X), but *mand* (2X) and *suan* (2X). None of these words varies in its spelling; thus, it is not the case that the variable rule is applying consistently across the lexicon, sensitive only to phonetic environment.

Although the *Corpus* shared glosses show a state of the language earlier than the nonshared sources and closer (as with *Erfurt*) to the archetype, it should be pointed out that *Corpus* and *Erfurt* vary independently. Both have *o* in 21 glosses, but *Erfurt* has *a* in 17 cases where *Corpus* has *o*, and, conversely, *o* in 8 cases where *Corpus* has *a*.[11] This observation is to be emphasized as it provides evidence that the variation in these texts represents synchronic variations in the language of the scribes rather than dialect mixture stemming from the textual tradition. Although none of the relationships in the *Erfurt* data is statistically significant, the differences between the texts are suggestive of later developments and can be summarized in the following variable rules:

Erfurt

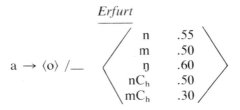

$$a \rightarrow \langle o \rangle / \underline{\quad} \left\{ \begin{array}{ll} n & .55 \\ m & .50 \\ ŋ & .60 \\ nC_h & .50 \\ mC_h & .30 \end{array} \right\}$$

[11] These data are summarized from H. M. Chadwick, "Studies in Old English," *Transactions of the Cambridge Philological Society* 4 (1894–1899): 200–204.

Corpus (shared)

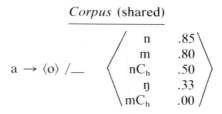

$$a \rightarrow \langle o \rangle /\!\!\underline{} \quad \left\langle \begin{array}{ll} n & .85 \\ m & .80 \\ nC_h & .50 \\ \eta & .33 \\ mC_h & .00 \end{array} \right\rangle$$

This presentation of the data helps emphasize the similarity of the development of the nasalized vowel in these two texts. The differences are what one would expect given the chronological relationship of the texts. Except for the glosses containing the velar nasal, the phonetic environments are found in the same implicational hierarchy in both texts: $n > m > nC_h > mC_h$. The divergence of the data /__η can be accounted for by the sparsity of the data for this environment. The independent *Corpus* data indicate an advanced sound change if not a completed one:

$$a \rightarrow \langle o \rangle /\!\!\underline{} \quad \left\langle \begin{array}{ll} {}^*m & \\ n & .75 \\ nC_h & .75 \\ \eta & .66 \\ mC_h & .66 \end{array} \right\rangle$$

A generalization of the variable rules demonstrates the relatedness of the texts even more strikingly:

$$a \rightarrow \langle o \rangle /\frac{}{[+\text{ nas}]} \langle + \text{ apical}\rangle \langle - \text{ seg}\rangle$$

What emerges is the picture of a sound change proceeding regularly, although variably, according to phonetic environment. The logical consequence of this direction of change is the state of the language to be seen in the *Vespasian Psalter*—where WGmc. *a* before nasals appears only as *o*. It is important to students of the language that variable data need not preclude, as it has for some,[12] meaningful analysis. That is, one may look at the following summaries of forms[13] and conclude that the texts from which they are drawn could not possibly represent the same dialect:

	Epinal	Erfurt	Corpus	Vesp. Psalter
a	58	32	38	none
o	1	33	95	all

Or, aided by a detailed analysis of the patterns of variation, one may conclude, as Kuhn suggested,[14] that the differences between the texts can be explained chronologically. Further, this analysis of the data argues strongly against attempts to attribute variation to dialect mixture or to the disparate dialects of the sources, as both of these would have resulted in a random distribution of *a* and *o*. This distribution is hardly random.

THE CHARTERS

From one point of view, however, the glossary data may perhaps present evidence of too regular a nature. That is, the number and nature of informants is severely limited. The glossaries cannot give us a cross section of the variety that was to be found in the non-homogeneous population of speakers of Mercian-dominated Old English. What is needed is a large collection of texts written in as

[12] For example, R. M. Wilson, "The Provenance of the Vespasian Psalter Gloss: The Linguistic Evidence," in *The Anglo-Saxons*, ed. P. Clemoes (London: Methuen, 1972).

[13] Because these numbers are based on my decisions about etymological values of the vowels in question and consequently differ from numbers reported by other scholars, the data on which they are based have been provided in full.

[14] Sherman M. Kuhn, "The Dialect of the Corpus Glossary," *PMLA* 54: 1–19.

many places and at as many times as possible. Although the historical linguist will of course take what he can get, in this case we are fortunate in that the charters fairly adequately meet this need. The most serious drawback of the charters is the limited extent to which Old English appears in them; were they more extensive, one could deal with the problems with greater confidence. The data from the Mercian charters are presented in what follows. For convenience words containing *a* spellings are placed finally and in parentheses.

736	(B-154)	*onoc*	(Worcs.)
759	(B-187)	*onnanforda, onnan* . *duun*	(Gloucs.)
779	(B-230)	*sulmonnes*	(Gloucs.)
788	(B-254)	*unuuano,* (*dunicgland*)	(Kent)
*793X796	(B-274)	*unu[u]ona*	(Gloucs.)
*798	(B-289)	*unuuono*	(Kent)
*799	(B-293)	*lond* (2X), *tomeworðige*	(Kent)
801	(B-201)	*unuuona*	(Middlesex)
803	(B-312)	*monn* (2X), *mon,* (*Dammucae*)	
805	(B-319)	*monn[a],* (*cudaman*)	(Kent)
*805	(B-321)	*Dudemon, ecgheannglond,* (*cantuuariorum*)	(Kent)
*805X807	(B-318)	*lond-* (5X), *mon* (*cantwariorum*)	(Kent)
*805X810	(B-330)	*aldormonn* (2X), *ond* (4X), *lond* (4X), *gesomnuncgae, on, monna, mon* (10X), *londe, ombra, hwonne, namon,* (*cantuarabyrg, man*)	(Kent)
808	(B-326)	*lond, tomeworðig*	(Kent)
*811	(B-332)	*folcuuininglond, on* (9X), *lond* (2X), *babinglond,* (*dunwalingland*)	(Kent)

*811	(B-335)	*appincglond, suiðhunicglond, aet grafonaea (mancosas)*	(Kent)
811	(B-339)	*(otanhyrst, crangbyras)*	(Kent)
*812	(B-341)	*ecgheanlond* (2X), *grafoneah, suiðhuniglond* (2X)	(Kent)
814	(B-343)	*hegeðonhyrs, sponleoge, long-, (anleag)*	(Kent)
*814	(B-348)	*lond, grafoneah* (2X), *seleberhtincglond, on* (2X)	(Kent)
*815	(B-353)	*seleberhtinglond, (mancusas)*	(Kent)
*822	(B-370)	*ondred-* (2X), *long, contwariorum (mancusas)*	(Kent)
*823	(B-374)	*londboc, (cantwariorum)*	(Kent)
*824	(B-378)	*on* (9X), *(lang)*	(Kent)
*825	(B-384)	*-homme, lond, boclonde, herefreðinglonde, on, (cantwarabyrg)*	(Middlesex and Kent)
*831	(B-400)	*monna, colanhomm*	(Middlesex)
*836	(B-416)	*lond* (6X)	(Worcs.)
*844X845	(B-452)	*monn, lond* (3X), *noman, (mancessan)*	(Bucks.)
*871X889	(B-536)	*onn, monie, mon* (4X), *ond* (7X), *hond, lond* (17X), *on, folclondes, boclondes, ealonde, sonderstede* (2X), *noman, (ann, and, manna, standað)*	(Kent)

The pre-700 charters hardly afford sufficient data to justify any meaningful conclusions. The first instance of *o* before a nasal in a southern manuscript occurs in the charter for 690X693 in the name *Hagona* (spelled *hagana* in two other contemporary charters). Otherwise, limited as they are, the early charters show *a*. References to the *cantuuariorum* occur frequently in the early data; here and elsewhere the word and its derivatives are excluded from word counts. As the data indicate a native Kentish spelling of *a* before nasals (see pages 93–95), one ought not to be surprised to find the people of Kent spelled *cantwara* throughout England.

Taken together, the 18 charters dating between A.D. 736 and 811 contain mostly *o* spellings (65 *o* versus 8 *a*). Twelve of these charters, including the six documents that are concerned with land outside of Kent, contain only the *o* graph. The six charters that do contain *a* are spread throughout the period: B-254 (788), B-312 (803), B-319 (805), B-330 (805X810), B-332 (811), and B-339 (811). Of these, two (B-254 and B-339) are consistent in having only *a*. It is worth noting that the Mercian letter forms are absent in these two MSS, and that both deal with land grants in Kent (3 of the 4 *a* forms are in Kentish place names). Documents B-312 (3 *o*, 1 *a*) and B-319 (1 *o*, 1 *a*) are also devoid of the letter forms; more interestingly, they are also both grants of land (in Kent) by the archbishop of Canterbury. The most important of these early documents are the fairly extensive ones—B-330 (805X810) and B-332 (811). In these MSS, which contain clear examples of Mercian letter forms, *o* predominates over occasional *a*s (B-330—26 *o*, 2 *a*; B-332—13 *o*, 1 *a*). It is clear that while *o* had become the regular spelling (and the sound change complete or near completion), it was still possible as late as 811 to find members of the Mercian speech community who would consistently write *a*.

The data from A.D. 812 to 845 argue for a completed sound change. Except for *lang*—B-378 (824)—, there are only *o* spellings: 47 *o*, 1 *a*. Even the Kentish folk are rendered *contwariorum*! If the sound change were not completed, the contemporary Latin borrowing, *mancus*, which first appears in A.D. 811 (B-335), would have been affected.

The Surrey document, B-536 (871X889), is testimony to the enduring effect of Mercian influence in southeast England. The *o* forms are 13 times as common as the *as* (39 *o*, 3 *a*). Data from the West Saxon–Kentish charters will help provide the details of Mercian influence. It is to be remembered that *o* is a nonnative spelling for both Kent and Wessex:

838	*Cot. Aug. ii 37*	*monnedi*
839	*Cot. Aug. ii 28* K²	*lond*
*845	*Cot. Aug. ii 60*	*longan, on, (-land, mancusas)*
847	*4Cot. Ch. viii 36*	*homme, on* (25X), *from* (3X), *non,* (*an* (2X), *fram*)
855	*Cot. Aug. ii 71*	(*landes* (2X))
858	*Cot. Aug. ii 66*	(*gang, an* (3X), *lamba, folcland* (2X), *land* (4X), *lamburnan, sandhyrst, landes*)
862	*Cot. Ch. viii 32* K²	*londe,* (*fram* (10X), *langan, nama* (3X))
863	*Cant. Ant. M 14*	*lond,* (*bocland, lande*)
*867	*Cot. Aug. ii 95*	(*mannel*)

There is a clear shift between A.D. 847 and 855. Before 847, *o* is dominant (35 *o*, 4 *a*). After 855, *o* becomes the occasional spelling (2 *o*, 36 *a*). Additional evidence for potential Mercian influence in charters of this general period comes from the presence of Mercian letter forms. Kuhn found several examples of Mercian *g* and *t* in *Cott. Aug. ii 60* and there are two *os* before a nasal. He only found a single Anglian *ð* in *Cott. Aug. ii 95*. Two of the West Saxon–Kentish charters (for 839 and 862) contain doubtful or compromise examples of the letters. Both have one *o* spelling. These findings corroborate the data from the "purely" Kentish charters: *o* spellings decline and finally disappear as Mercian influence recedes.

THE MINOR TEXTS

Of the *Minora*, only the *Lorica Prayer*, the *Lorica Glosses*, the *Blickling Glosses*, and the *Omont Leaf* can be dated within the period of Mercian political dominance. The earliest, the *Blickling*

Glosses, has only two relevant words: *granode* and *from,* but these occur in the mixture of forms to be expected in an early text. The material from the *Book of Cerne* is quite different. Only *o* is found:

Lorica Prayer: monn, from, noman
Lorica Glosses: heafudponnan (2X), *honda, heorthoman,*
lichoman, homme, on[d]wlite, sconcum

The *Omont Leaf* exhibits only *o* spellings of the nasalized vowel: *ðone* (2X), *on* (3X), *gemong, ðonne, sconcan.*

The remaining Mercian texts all belong to the period after the decline of Mercian authority. This fact is particularly important since none of them can be dated or localized with certainty. The most extensive of the texts are the glosses to the *Cotton Tiberius C ii* and two fragments of the Anglo-Saxon *Martyrology, B. M. Additional MSS 23211* and *40165,* all s. ix/x. The Bede MS (*Cot. Tib. C ii*) contains both inked and scratched glosses. The inked glosses belong to the late ninth century; the scratches are the work of at least two scribes. The hand of one of these scribes is nearly contemporary with that of the Latin texts (s. viii); the other is perhaps tenth century. The work of differentiating between the hands of the two glossators is yet to be done. In the glosses of the late ninth century, WGmc. **a* before nasals is regularly *o.*

> *compdomes*
> *nomementa*
> *lond*
> *onlicnis*
> *on* (twice)
> *[h]omme*

There are three cases of *a* in the scratched glosses but *o* is by far the commoner (40 *o,* 3 *a*):

a: *utgange*   *bocland*   *hafudpenne*

112

The Charters

o:

frinomon	*[o]neardan*	*onwalda*
onfunden hron	*galdrmonum*	*onmunenne*
monnes	*ealonde*	*tongan*
onwalde	*lond*	*gesomnunge*
onhyrgan	*aldermon*	*onefn*
compe	*gesomnede*	*ongeat*
ongin	*doncful*	*monigheoulice*
onwald	*onhyrgan*	
we[p]nedmonnes	*wongum*	
onwece	*ongeotan*	
on (3X)	*gelomp*	
	ond (2X)	
	on (5X)	

The *Martyrology Fragments* contain only *o:*

Add. 23211	Add. 40165
mon (3X)	*ongon* (2X)
noma (3X)	*on* (14X)
monnes	*hond*
gesponnan	*monn* (7X)
monigra	*monnes* (3X)
hond	*monnum* (4X)
hwon	*ontyned*
somod	*noman*
ond	*lichoman* (11X)
monncwild	*from*
on	*forðgonge*
	ond (6X)
	onfon
	onsione
	on
	sond
	hondum
	hongade
	stronggestan
	ondrysnlice (2X)

113

The inscription to the *Codex Aureus* contains only one *a* against seven *o* spellings:

a	*o*
man	mon
	to ðoncunca
	aldormon
	ond
	stondan
	from
	noman

LATER TEXTS

Three texts, although they fall outside of the period of the main sources for this study, merit consideration as they show later developments of the sound change now being considered. The first of these are glosses to a late eighth-century prayer book (*B. M. Royal 2 A. xx*). The glosses themselves are assigned on paleographical grounds to the first part of the tenth century[15] and were first printed by Zupitza,[16] the source of the data reproduced here. Nasal *a* is represented as *o* except in two words—*fram* and *andre* (glossing *et*)—which usually are not fully stressed (42 *o*, 2 *a*):

noma, -n (2X)	onseone	gonge
fro(m (5X)	ondwlite	hondum, -a (3X)
on (14X)	forþon (3X)	forgonges
lichoman (2X)	onfeong	þon
onsiene	ðonne	onæled (3X)
		honccrede (2X)

[15] E. A. Lowe, *Codices Latini Antiquiores* (Oxford: Oxford University Press, 1935), p. 28.

[16] Julius Zupitza, "Mercisches aus der Hs. Royal 2 A 20 im Britischen Museum," *Zeitschrift für Deutsches Altertum* 33 (1889): 47–66.

If this is a Worcester MS, as most believe,[17] it demonstrates the linguistic continuity necessary to explain the *o* before nasals found in Middle English MSS of the West Midlands.

The interlinear gloss to the *Rushworth Gospels* (*Bod. Auct. D. 2. 19*) is a rarity among OE MSS; we know when, where, and by whom it was made. The Mercian portion, called *Rushworth*[1], was made by Farmon, a priest, at Harewood about 975. Kuhn has demonstrated that his language is basically Mercian with hypercorrections toward the politically dominant West Saxon.[18] With the exception of Brown,[19] who lists all of the examples in his dissertation, commentators on the language of the *Rushworth* glosses have felt it sufficient to say that WGmc. *a before nasals appears as *o* about six times more frequently than it does as *a*. That statistic, however, is misleading; the complete data follow.

$$/—\eta$$

a	*o*
gang (5X)	*gongan* (3X)
gangan (52X)	*longe* (2X)
lange (2X)	

$$/—m$$

a	*o*
gelamp (3X)	*gelomp* (19X)
	fro(m (76X)
	somed
	tosomne (3X)
	somnaþ (3X)
	gesomnade
	somnunge (41X)

[17] Neil R. Ker, *Catalogue of Manuscripts Containing Anglo-Saxon* (Oxford: Oxford University Press, 1957), p. 318.

[18] Sherman M. Kuhn, ''*e* and *æ* in Farman's Mercian Glosses,'' *PMLA* 60 (1945): 631–669.

[19] Edward Miles Brown, *Die Sprache der Rushworth Glossen zum Evangelium Matthäus und der mercische Dialeckt* (I. *Vokale*) (Göttingen: W. Fr. Kästner, 1891), pp. 18–19.

/__m

a	o
	wombe (2X)
	hwommes (2X)
	noma (12X)
	loma (4X)

/__n

a	o
an	*on* (94), *þone* (47X)
man	*onseone*
blan	*mon* (Pro) (2X)
panne	*mon(n* (113X)
forþan	*con(n* (4X)
þanne (22X)	*wona*
hwanne (3X)	*þonan* (16X)
and- (14X)	*þon* (11X)
standende	*forþon* (31X)
bewand	*þonne* (Conj) (65X)
candel-	*þonne* (7X)
ongan (2X)	*hwonne* (2X)
ingann	*ond*
geþanc	*ond-* (52X)
þane (Pro) (4X)	*hond* (30X)
	lond (27X)
	sond
	gebond
	monde (2X)
	stondende (3X)
	stondan (9X)
	ongon
	ingonn (5X)
	hona (2X)
	monade (2X)
	monig (42X)
	monunge
	þongunge (2X)
	forðoncum

The following summary of data indicates that the principal sources of *a* spellings are the environments of a following *n* or *ng* (phonetic [ŋg]):

	-*m*	-*n*	-*ng*
o	162 (98%)	593 (90%)	5 (9%)
a	3	56	59

In fact, all of the *a*s before *m* occur before *m* plus a homorganic consonant and 87% (47 of 56) of the *a*s before *n* are found in weakly stressed words. As it is the weakly stressed words which retain *o* spellings in West Saxon, these *a* spellings are another instance of Farmon's tendency to hypercorrect. Taking these refinements into consideration, the statistics become:

	/__m	/__mC$_h$	/´__n	/´__nC$_h$	/__n	/__ŋ
o	141	21	246	73	247	5
a	0	3	9	4	47	59

The data can be restated as a variable rule:

$$a \rightarrow \langle o \rangle\ /\underset{\smile}{\overset{\prime}{\underline{\hspace{1em}}}}\ \left\langle \begin{array}{ll} \text{*m} & \\ \text{\_\_n} & .97 \\ \text{nC}_h & .95 \\ \text{mC}_h & .88 \\ \text{\_\_n} & .84 \\ \text{ŋ} & .09 \end{array} \right\rangle$$

While the variable rule offers a convenient means of summarizing patterns of variation, it is interesting as well to look at the sound change's effect in individual lexical items. For example, *o* becomes *a* in unstressed positions before [n] an average of 16% of the time. But *on* is spelled *an* only once out of 95 occurrences; *þone* is spelled *þane* 8% of the time. In 22 of 94 cases, *þonne* is found as *þanne*. Clearly, the lexicon is not affected uniformly on the basis of phonetic environment. The language is changing one word at a time; Farmon's

117

spellings show that he retains and loses certain West Saxon pronunciations on a word-to-word basis.

POLITICAL MOTIVATION OF SOUND CHANGE

The evidence reported here provides an opportunity to monitor the progress of the development of WGmc. *a before nasal consonants throughout the period of its change from a to o. The sound change probably began in the north and diffused through the Mercian speech community during the years of Mercian dominance of England. The earliest text studied (the *Epinal Glossary*) is unaffected by the change. The other glossaries contain data that are understandable if viewed as mirroring the chronological development of a to o. In fact, the material that is peculiar to the *Corpus Glossary* would argue for completion of the sound change by the turn of the eighth century. A consideration of the charters makes it possible to date the sound change more accurately. Between A.D. 803 and 824, the Kentish–Mercian charters have only o. Thus the sound change must have been complete (or been viewed as complete by the Kentish). The o spelling predominates in Mercian charters from A.D. 736 on, and is found exclusively from A.D. 812 to 845. In addition to establishing an early dating for the sound change, the data from these varying sources provide insight into the processes by which linguistic change occurs. The change began variably in a small subset of the lexicon and diffused through the lexicon on a word-by-word basis but sensitive to phonetic environment. The charter data, further, give evidence for the heterogeneous progress of the change through the Mercian speech community: Some speakers could write a as late as 811 (the sporadic a spellings in the late ninth-century MSS are probably due to the influence of West Saxon, the language of the politically dominant). Of more global interest is the fact that Mercian political domination could effect linguistic change in Kent. From the time of the earliest recorded sound changes, language and politics, literacy and the political–social establishment, have been intertwined.

4

Conspiracy and Competition in the Implementation of Language Change

MONG the most volatile sounds in the whole history of the English language is /æ/ that developed from West Germanic *a;* its subsequent development is surely among the most difficult to describe. The history of the backed allophone, and its variation between *a* and *o* before nasals, was relatively simple to discuss because the environment in which it occurred was highly restricted and easily stated. On the other hand, the fronted allophone—that is, Old English *æ*— was found in a wide range of phonetic environments, and was consequently subject to a number of different influences, only some of which resulted in permanent language change. As a further complication, the phonetic environments for different sound changes were not always discrete; when they overlapped, competition among sound changes resulted. In addition to the nasal development already treated, early Old English *æ*, variously spelled *ae*, *æ*, and *ę* (*e-caudata*), was subject to the following conditioned changes:

1. It was retracted to a back vowel, spelled *a*, before a back segment—a back vowel in the following syllable, a velar consonant (not the fricative), or a velarized consonant group (*w* and *l* plus a consonant). This generalization subsumes several independent phenomena that will be scrutinized in what follows.
2. It was regularly diphthongized (in philological terms, underwent breaking) to [æə], spelled *ea*, when it occurred before *r* plus a consonant, or the velar spirant, spelled *c*, *g*, *h*.
3. The diphthong so produced was subsequently monophthongized (smoothed) before χ, alone or in combinations with *r* (*rc*, *rg*,

120

rh), back to a vowel spelled *æ*. A change of place of articulation from velar [χ] to palatal [ç] would help account for the first breaking, then smoothing effect of the spirant. Unfortunately, there is no orthographic evidence for such a change.

4. A prehistoric process known as *i-umlaut*—the fronting of back vowels (or raising of front vowels) conditioned by a following high, front segment—could affect the development of:
   (a) the *æ* produced by the general fronting of West Germanic *a.
   (b) West Germanic *a before nasals.
   (c) Old English *æ* in the breaking environments.
   (d) the *a* produced by retraction before *l*C.
   (e) the *æ* in the first breaking, then smoothing environment of the velar (later perhaps palatal) spirant.

The *æ*s that were unaffected by any of the preceding changes underwent an unconditioned raising to a vowel spelled *e;* the process is unhappily termed the second fronting.

The situation is clearly a highly complex one, and the problems related to dating and interpreting the interactions between such a set of competing changes are enormous. As might be imagined, Anglo-Saxonists have maintained a variety of views on the subject. In fact, the following discussion implies a chronological ordering of these changes that differs from the standard handbook presentation.[1] The reevaluation of the chronology is an important aspect of this study but can be discussed and defended only after a complete presentation of the data. The discussion of the data is facilitated by separate treatment of these etymologically different developments. The separation, for example, of the *æ* produced by i-umlaut of nasalized *a* and the *æ* produced by smoothing may at first seem an unnecessary mixing of diachrony and synchrony. However, because these *æ*s developed quite differently, there is good reason to suppose

---

[1] A. Campbell, *Old English Grammar* (Oxford: Oxford University Press, 1959), pp. 105–110, offers a summary discussion of the received view of the chronology of the early sound changes.

that language history was reflected in synchrony. Though similar enough to spell with one graph, the two *æ*s differed subtly, perhaps imperceptibly, in their pronunciation. Thus *æ* before nasals was probably higher, more fronted (possibly tenser) than *æ* before the velar fricative. Such differences are understandable in terms of phonetic motivation and help explain why the first sound was subject to raising whereas the second was not. During the period under study, the raised *æ*s began to be perceived as closer to [ɛ] and became variably spelled with *e*.

The early glossaries contain a few forms in which the regular fronting of [a] to [æ] seems to have been blocked (or in which the fronted vowel became retracted). These forms will be considered before we proceed to a detailed analysis of the variety of forms to be found for the developments of WGmc. **a*. In six glosses in the *Epinal Glossary*, *a* is found before a front vowel in the following syllable: *auuel, cladersticca, nabae, habern, gladinae, quatern.* Some of these words are repeated in the same form in the *Erfurt* and *Corpus Glossaries: Erfurt—hafern, quaterni, auuel; Corpus— clader, awel. Corpus* adds *laser* to the list. Retraction (or failure of fronting) before [w] is well attested,[2] and, understandably, the bilabial fricative [β] had the same effect, accounting for *nabae, habern*, etc. That the retraction was variable is evidenced by such forms as *Corpus haebrn* and *haebern.* The forms *clader* and *cladersticca* are not really exceptions as they derive from *cladur-.* It is not uncommon to find unstressed back vowels written *e* in the early texts; and, as we will see in what follows, the vowel so written was real enough to cause velar umlaut (the diphthongization of front vowels caused by a back vowel in the immediately following syllable). The remaining words, *quatern, gladinae, laser*, etc., are Latin loan words. Their form in these very early texts may still reflect Latin spelling; however, in later glossaries and elsewhere in Old English, they occur with *æ* and *e*. We are left with the interesting suggestion that the environment that induced retraction had earlier been (at least variably) more general.

[2] Campbell, *Grammar*, p. 55.

122

WEST GERMANIC *a BEFORE rC

The normal diphthongal development to [æə] (written *ea*) was probably complete by A.D. 700. Of 24 possible cases in *Epinal*, *ea* is found in 22 glosses. The exceptions are *sparuua* and *geruuae*. One is tempted to attribute the variation to scribal error—in each case, the omission of a letter. If so, the spelling apparently stems from the *Erfurt–Epinal* archetype; the glosses appear identically in both MSS.

The *Erfurt Glossary* further attests breaking in the language of the *Epinal–Erfurt* archetype. The vowel in question is spelled *ea* in 17 out of 32 possible cases. As the manuscript was copied by an Old High German scribe whose native speech would not have a diphthong in this environment, the scribe can be expected to "correct" the unfamiliar readings of his exemplar and its foreign (Anglo-Saxon) words. We can take his *ea* spellings as stronger than usual evidence of those forms in the *Epinal–Erfurt* archetype; that is, evidence that breaking was complete before the copying of the *Epinal Glossary*.

The following graphs are found in addition to the 17 examples of the expected *ea:*

æ	a	e
aerngeup	foetribarn	stern
stẹrn	ediscuard	wernuislicæ
uaertae	uuard	uuertae
	uard	felufrech
	sparua	merth
		geruẹ
		bẹcdermi

To these should be added the garbled *fiindi* (for *gearnwinde*). Although the high incidence of scribal errors in these data does not inspire confidence, the data are not completely chaotic. In fact, these errors are in themselves quite suggestive. We find here, as we do elsewhere

123

in the *Erfurt Glossary*, mistakes that a scribe, especially a nonnative scribe, might make if he were copying from an exemplar in which the Old English glosses were scratched with a dry point rather than inked. Not only are scratched glosses difficult to read (accounting for confusions not easily explained by similarities in letter forms), but they are often limited to only as much of the word as the original scribe thought necessary to call the word to mind. Thus the copier would be left to fill in the gaps. An incompletely scratched *ftrbrn* might then yield the confused *foetribarn* for the intended *fosturbearn*, and a totally confused *fiindi* could thereby arise.

In 3 of the 30 cases of WGmc. **a/ __rC*, we find what appears to be an unbroken *æ*. This at once suggests that there was still some variation in the archetype which the *Epinal* scribe modernized to his dialect, but which the *Erfurt* scribe copied faithfully. The alternate hypothesis that the *æ* represents the i-umlaut product of either [æə] or retracted [a] must be rejected. *Epinal earngeut* and *stearno* along with *Corpus earngeot, stearn, wearte* (all deriving from the archetype) show no sign of i-umlaut. Even more interestingly, seven glosses have an *e* for the expected *ea*. Chadwick, strangely enough, does not mention the alternation. Dieter, whose main object, after all, is the language of the *Epinal* and *Corpus Glossaries*, merely notes it as an example of dialect interference which precludes meaningful analysis:

> Aus den schreibungen *uuertae* v 1. *uaertae* b 65. *aerngeup* a 137 (= Ep. 2 b 21). *foetribarn* a 238 u. s. w. darf man bei dem hd. schreiber, der den laut *ea* garnicht kannte, keine schlüsse ziehen.[3]

Given that the *ea* spelling was unfamiliar to a speaker of Old High German, it is possible that the *æ* and *e* spellings are attributable to the Erfurt scribe's attempt to make sense of his exemplar—when in doubt he would modify what he saw by dropping a letter or transposing letters. That the diphthongal spellings confused him is

---

[3] Ferdinand Dieter, *Ueber Sprache und Mundart der ältesten englischen Denkmäler* (Göttingen: Academische Buchhandlung von G. Calvör, 1885), p. 35.

further evident from the three false metatheses which split up the unfamiliar clusters: *feran, duæram, erabedlica*.

Although one cannot base an argument on data copied by a nonnative speaker of English, these data are not unexplainable. In three of five cases the retracted vowel is found in a syllable (-*ward*) that is a common element in personal names. We know of the role which Northumbrian religious played in the establishment of continental centers of learning. Retraction of *æ* before *r*C is a regular feature of Northumbrian varieties of Old English, and a feature of Old English phonology that an Old High German scribe would know from his daily commerce with Englishmen. The regularity with which unbroken *æ* is spelled *e* is not likely attributable to error in copying. This scribe is probably recording the fact that the Old English speakers of his acquaintance regularly substituted an [ε]-like sound for his own *a*. The agreement of Epinal *geruuae* with Erfurt *geruę* argues that unbroken [æ] raised to [ε] was to be found in the language of their common source.

The data from the *Leyden Glossary* are very interesting when viewed alongside those from *Erfurt*. Breaking is not found; the Northumbrian (or nonnative) retraction is more common (5 examples out of 12). There is further evidence of raising (3 of 7 nonretracted *æ*s are spelled *e*) in the continental community of Old English speakers:

æ	*e*	*a*
maerth	herma	uarras
sneðildaerm	herst	uarras
uaert[a]e	erm	arngeus
haerd		darmana
		harperi

There are a total of 59 glosses in the *Corpus Glossary* that contain a vowel developed from WGmc. *a* before *r*C. The vast majority show a vowel cluster represented by the expected orthographic convention for [æa]—48 examples with *ea* (including two glosses with *eo* which was early confused with *ea*). There is one example of unbroken *æ*, along with two examples of unbroken *æ* raised to *e*. Seven glosses exhibit a retracted vowel: *bisparrade, barricgae, barice, sarwo, tharme, þuarm, neoþouard*. These last examples are further evidence of a Northumbrian presence recorded in the common archetype of these three early glossaries.

Breaking is the rule in the *Vespasian Psalter*; it is found in over 400 glosses with only occasional exceptions. The exceptions are, however, interesting. In four cases we find confusion of *eo* and *ea: eordunge, ðiorfan, beorn, beorna;* once, the archaic spelling *hæarmcweodelien*. The *eo* and *ea* spellings reflect, of course, a confusion of the first element of the diphthong, not the second. That is, [ɛ] and [æ] are confused, not surprising in texts in which these sounds were falling together. Four examples with *-erC* (*erð, bern, bernu(m, ferra*) reflect the scribe's uncertainty, as do three more examples in which this careful scribe corrected his errors and added an *a* above the line—*e*ᵃ*rð, be*ᵃ*rn, awe*ᵃ*rp*. These would be negligible if it were not for the evidence from the glossaries for an early raising of unbroken *æ*.

Except for one gloss (*feoluferð, Lorica Glosses*), which probably shows the effects of i-umlaut, the minor texts regularly show breaking / __*r*C. The Latin names in the Mercian copy of Bede depart consistently from the Northumbrian copies: *suᶒheardo, uuigheard, bearuae*. A. Campbell inexplicably refers to the last example as one of the "instances from early North. texts where breaking occurs despite a labial consonant"[4] (he elsewhere wishes to consider the text Kentish[5] or Mercian).[6] Other examples of breaking from the *Minora* are:

Lorica Prayer: *geearingum, middangeardes*
Lorica Glosses: *ðearmgewind, smælðearmus, snᶒdelðearm*
Bede Glosses: *earfedðnisse, searwe, scearplice, earm* (3X);
                 (scratched) *searacræft* (sic), *swearm*

[4] Campbell, *Grammar*, p. 56.
[5] Ibid., p. 8.
[6] A. Campbell, review of *The Life of St. Chad*. by R. Vleeskruyer, *Medium Ævum* 24 (1955): 55.

Codex Aureus: ðearfe
Martyrology: hearde (B. M. Add. MS 23211) all (B. M. Add. MS 40165A)
Royal Glosses: eart (2X), earm- (2X), middangeardes

The broad spectrum of data from the charters confirms the state of the language attested in the various other sources. The major deviation from regular breaking is to be seen in personal names (in what follows, nonbroken forms are indicated with parentheses).

736	(B-154)	*heardberht*
*742	(B-162)	*he[a]rdberht*
788	(B-254)	*heardraed*
*793X796	(B-274)	*heardberht, æðelheardi, alhheardi*
*798	(B-289)	*aedelhard, heardberhti, (alhhard)*
801	(B-201)	*heardberht, æthelheardus, alhheard, pilheardus*
803	(B-312)	*alhheard, notheard, wigheard, uulfheard (2X), wulfheard, aeðelheardus (2X), (wighard)*
*803	(B-310)	*æðelheardus (4X), æðelheardo, uulfheardus, alhheardus*
*805	(B-321)	*heardberht, beornheard, alh[i]ardi, uuigheard, uulfheardi, aeðilgeard, (uulfhardo, ceoluuard)*
*805X807	(B-318)	*alhheard, wulfheard, æðeliard*
808	(B-326)	*heardberht, biornheardes, (ceolward)*
*805X810	(B-330)	*gegearwien, reogalweord, (reogolwarde, towardon)*
*811	(B-335)	*heardberht*
*811	(B-332)	*aeðelheard (2X), badaheard, billheard, uulfheard, wynnbearding, eangeard, (brunhard)*
811	(B-339)	*heardberht*
*812	(B-341)	*sighearingmeduue*
814	(B-343)	*cært, beardingaleag, wilheard, heardberht, wigheard, (wulfhard, earlhhard, wighard)*

*814	(B-348)	bearwe, heardberhti, uuigheardi
*822	(B-370)	beadheard, wulfheard
*823	(B-374)	beadheard
*824	(B-378)	alchheard, suðeuueardan, fearn
*825[7]	(B-384)	(brunhard, coenhard, cynehard, alchard, wærhard)
*831	(B-400)	(æðelhard)
836	(B-416)	(æþelhard, ecghard)
844	(B-452)	ecgheard
*873	(B-536)	midearðe, earduulf, erfeweard, erfewearda, erfeweardum, forðweard, (onwardum, towardan)

The charters of the earliest Mercian kings, Æðelbald and Offa, although limited, regularly show breaking to ea. Of the remaining 22 charters, only 10 exhibit ea exclusively. An additional 9 vary between ea and a, with a found 28% of the time. Occasional spellings with retracted vowels in names can be explained by the presence of Northumbrian religious in the heterogeneous religious community of early Anglo-Saxon times. A Northumbrian's name might be spelled with an a by a scrupulous scribe; a Northumbrian scribe might inadvertently so spell the names of others. Variation begins during the troubled reign of Cenwulf, especially in the documents associated with Canterbury and Æðelheard, the archbishop and Wulfred, his erstwhile archdeacon (later himself archbishop). Æðelheard is often spelled Æðelhard and even Æðeliard. Both spellings show a decided Northumbrian flavor, not unexpected in the name of the one-time abbot of Louth. There is a possibility that the a spellings represent a Latin influence—there is no ea or eo in Latin.

In the analysis of the names of church worthies in the early charters, one is constantly reminded of the heterogeneity of the early English ecclesiastical community. That a Northumbrian element was well established in Canterbury can further be seen in the names of the moneyers who served the kingdoms of Mercia and Kent:

---

[7] Both copies of this charter (Cott. Aug. ii 78 and Stowe 15) agree on these forms.

West Germanic *a before rC

Offa: *celhard, ciolard, banhard, beahheard (beanneard?),*
            bęghard
Cœnwulf: *suuefherd, uerheardi, werheard, ceolhard, wighard*

There is no doubt that these coins were struck at Canterbury.[8] A mixture of forms, especially in personal names, is to be expected in the productions of the learned communities whose members were drawn from all parts of England. The extent to which the variation is minimized is testimony to the strength of the influence of the Mercian kings and religious.

There is considerable evidence for an early (pre-700) metathesis of *r* in the texts being considered here. In many cases the metathesized *r* has returned to its original position, but the influence of the process is still to be observed. The diachronic and synchronic relationships of metathesis to breaking are interesting. Forms in which there is a destruction of the breaking environment would require that metathesis either preceded the breaking historically or was synchronically ordered before breaking. That is, breaking is inhibited in these forms. That it was at least contemporary with breaking and outlived it as a viable synchronic process can be seen in those forms in which a breaking environment is produced but in which no breaking ever occurs. It is interesting that metathesis always works to bleed breaking. The relevant examples are as follows:

Epinal	Erfurt	Corpus
		graes
baers	*baers*	*bre[r]s*
	gręs-	*graes-*
uuinaern	*uuinaern*	*winaern*

Bede Glosses: *bærnde,* and the scratched *hern* (for *ern*)
Blickling Psalter: *hordern*
Vespasian Psalter: *gershoppe, ern* (2X)
Martyrology: *-bęrnde*

---

[8] George C. Brooke, *English Coins* (London: Methuen & Co., 1950), pp. 18–19.

The high incidence of unbroken [æ] in the early glossaries can probably be attributed to the fact that metathesis was a strong productive element in early Mercian phonology. The regularity of breaking and metathesis suggests that both were complete before A.D. 700.

WEST GERMANIC *a BEFORE lC

In the Anglian dialects (occasionally in early West Saxon and Kentish), West Germanic *a is represented as a before lC. The texts of this study are not exceptional in this regard. Variation from the norm is truly sporadic and is found only in the charters. It seems pointless to reproduce here pages of regular data, but the following deviations are noteworthy:

679 (B-45)	*aeldredi*
736 (B-154)	*edilbalt, aethilbalt, aethilbaldo, aetdilbalt, ethibaldi, ealduuft*
812 (B-341)	*suuealuue*

The first example is important because it provides evidence—however meager—that the sound in question passed through a fronted state—approximately [æ]. The retraction to *a* is so regular that one might otherwise suppose that the general fronting of West Germanic *a* to Primitive Old English *æ* was inhibited by / __lC. One would expect, however, that West Saxon *eal* __lC ([æə]) developed from a fronted [æ] rather than a retracted vowel. The other two very minor exceptions to the rule are further evidence that the presence of West Saxons in the Anglo-Saxon religious communities was felt even though it was generally suppressed during the Mercian era.

130

THE EFFECTS OF i-UMLAUT

That i-umlaut was a relatively early sound change is attested by the fact that Primitive Old English *$æ$ from West Germanic *a is with few exceptions represented e when it occurs in i-umlaut positions. I-umlaut was variably hindered in Primitive Old English by two groups of consonant clusters, fC and sC. From the *Epinal Glossary* we have *staef endra, gistaebn endre, anheabd, feast-* (2X), *aesc, maestun* BUT *eordestae* and *restaendum*. The tendency is too regular to attribute to analogical restoration of $æ$, as does Campbell.[9] Indeed, if there is leveling at all, it is in the direction of extending the umlauted vowel into inhibited environments. Thus, we find $æ$ only before sC in the *Vespasian Psalter*, but the influence is waning and the lexical subset of *feste* and its compounds are always spelled with e. The remaining examples are evenly split between $æ$ and e.

When i-umlaut affected the West Germanic *a before -rC, the sound produced was usually written e in non-West Saxon texts. The earliest Mercian texts exhibit an interesting alternation. The following data are taken from the glossaries:

Epinal: *gegeruuednae, gigeruuid, sercae, uuergendi, heruuendlicae, tochgerd, ferhergend, fertd,* but *segilgaerd*

Erfurt: *gegeruedne, fohergend, sercae, gerd, auuerdid,* but *haeruendlicae, segilgaerd*

Corpus: *forhergend, werdit, huerbende, hergiung, huerbende, serce, gegeruuid, huerb, awendid, wergendi, erdling, seruuende, ferdun, gerd* (3X), *mersc, gegaerwendne, gierende,* but *gewaerpte, faerd, -gærd* (2X)

The regularity with which this sound is represented $æ$ in the early texts suggests that the umlauted sound passed through a stage of [æ] on its way to becoming [ɛ]. This means that the i-umlaut of a

---

[9] Campbell, *Grammar*, p. 76.

or broken *ea* was for a time [æ]. Perhaps a more plausible explanation is that breaking was hindered by the conditioning factor that caused i-umlaut. It is, after all, generally recognized that an *i* in the next syllable prevented breaking in a number of environments: *-ewe* from **æwi; -iwe* from **iwi;* in Anglia, of *i/ __rCi;* in non-West Saxon dialects, of *e/ __χi.* The variation in the glossaries is then to be explained as variable raising of unbroken [æ].

There are several rather late examples in which the i-umlaut of **a/ __rC* is represented with *æ:*

	844X845 (B-452)	*erfe* (3X), *incerre*
BUT		
	873 (B-536)	*erfeweard-*(3X)

The *Vespasian Psalter* has only forms with *e;* there are no examples in the minor texts. Both *Chad* and *Rushworth*[1], late Mercian texts, have several instances of *æ:* 3 of 16 and 6 of 27, respectively. The examples from *Rushworth*[1], especially, may represent back-spellings resulting from the general confusion of [æ] and [ɛ] from any source.

It is important to observe that the data from the early texts argue strongly that i-umlaut was not a productive sound change in early Old English. First, the sound change is usually opaque; the conditioning factor has been destroyed. More important, perhaps, is the fact that when an unaccented *i* does appear, the vowel of the preceding syllable is never umlauted: *-heardi,* and hundreds of examples like it.

Primitive Old English **æ,* when retracted to *a* in the environment preceding *l*C, was subject to i-umlaut, yielding *æ:*

Epinal: *blestbaelf, bitui[c]n, aeldrum, caelith, aelbitu, unamaelti, onhaelði*

Erfurt: *blestbaelg, ældrum, cælid, cucaelf, cinamelti,* BUT *oheldi, elbitu*

Corpus: *blestbaelg, aeldrum, kaelið, aelbitu, unamaelte, ohældi, bloestbaelg, aelbitu, aeldra faeder, aelding, taelg, hindcaelf, faelging, faelging, afael, aeldra, ae[l]den, caelf, cucaelf, herbid* (sic)

It is, of course, impossible to determine if these glosses represent the i-umlauted product of a retracted vowel or if the umlauting *i* caused retraction to fail. Apparently retraction did not occur before *ll* formed as a result of West Germanic consonant gemination. The *i* which caused gemination umlauted (raised) the nonretracted vowel to *e: scel, ellaen, uelyrgae, eduuella*, etc. from all glossaries. The raising of the umlauted (or nonretracted) vowel to *e* is seen to a limited extent in the *Erfurt Glossary* (and in the corrupted *herbid* of the *Corpus Glossary*). This raising anticipates the change which was to be common to all Old English dialects and is reflected in Middle English developments to *e* (except in the West Midlands where the *æ* remains and develops into Middle English *a*). The beginning of this change is typically seen in *Rushworth*[1], and the *e*s found in *Erfurt* may well be part of the general falling together of *æ* and *e* from any source. The *Vespasian Psalter* and *Chad* both retain only *æ* spellings, whereas *Rushworth*[1] has *e* in 11 of 28 possible cases. The *Omont Leaf* has one example, *wælc*. There are occasional relevant forms scattered throughout the charters. The charter for A.D. 822 (B-370) has *welle* (the *Vespasian Psalter* has *welle* in two of nine occurrences) but the document for A.D. 831 (B-400) has the expected *mercwælle* and *botewælle* (2X). The form *elmessan* is found in the charter for A.D. 873 (B-536) and in several of the Mercian-influenced "Kentish" charters—Sweet Nos. 30, 39, and 40.

As was seen in the previous chapter of this study, West Germanic **a* had a special development before nasal consonants. The i-umlaut product of **a* before nasals is interesting in several respects. At first the sound was written as expected, *æ*, but there was a very early tendency to write the sound *e*. That the sound was not regularly fronted is seen in its usual alternation between *a* and *o*. The mutation to *æ* and subsequent raising to *e* adds plausibility to the suggested parallel developments of West Germanic **a* before *rCi* and *lCi*, in which the vowel had for a time an [ɛ]-like quality. The umlauted vowel—except for one example, *oembecht*, in the *Corpus Glossary*—is always written *æ* or *e*. If the nasal *a/o* alternation had been established before i-umlaut was complete, we would expect to find *œ* and *æ* in proportions correlating with the distribution of *o* and *a* before nasals. The *Corpus oembecht* can be explained as a back-spelling since both [œ] and [æ] were falling together under [ɛ]. The raising of the umlaut product to *e* appears to have been complete by the time that the *Corpus Glossary* was written:

Epinal: *dopaenid, aenid, aemil, faengae, graennung, lẹndino, aend-, gimaengiungiae, caempan, gigrẹmid, oberuuaendae, giuuaemmid, gemaengdae, feruuaenid, graemid, gigraemid, edischaen, gifraemith, gifraemid, laempihalt, lẹndnum,* BUT *stegn* (sic), *anhendi, gimengilicẹ, fremu, menigio, menescillingas, lectinadl*

Erfurt: *dopaenid, aenit, aemil, faengae, graemung, stẹng, anhaendi, gimaengidlicæ, æmil, laendum,* BUT *lendino, end-, gimengungae, cempan, gigremit, oberuendedæ, geuemmid, gimengdæ, feruendid, gremid, gigremid, -henim, gifremit, lemphihalt, meniscillingas, lectin, fremu, lebuendi, cempa, lenlibreda*

Corpus: *dopaenid, laendino, gemẹngan,* wodhae (sic), BUT *enid, emil, fendge, grennung, end-, gemengiunge, cempan, gegremid, oberuuenide, ungeuuemmid, gemengde, foruuened, gremið, gegremid, -hen, gefremið, gefremid, hemphalt, steng, anhendi, gemengetlic, emil, mene-, lenctin-, fre[o]mo,*[10] *ellende, wyrtdrenc, fraetgengian, werna, menget, suenceth, end-, meniu, endistaeb, uulencu, naectgenge, gemenged, genge, gremman, lendebrede, fremmendum, fremid, meremenin, benc, ablendeð, awenide, geuuendit, seng, menen*

As a preliminary observation, notice how rarely the umlauting *i* is preserved. The chronological development can be emphasized in the following tabular summary of the data:

[10] This gloss shows the effects of subsequent velar umlaut.

Smoothing

	Epinal	*Erfurt*	*Corpus*
æ	21	10	4
e	7	21	49

Considering that the Corpus scribe's exemplar would contain a high percentage of *æ*s, the 93% incidence of *e*s certainly points to a completed sound change, whose progress is recorded at two earlier stages in *Epinal* and *Erfurt*.

The *æ* is preserved in names in the Mercian MS of Bede,[11] but the remaining texts of this study show the completed raising to *e*. There are, of course, exceptions of a minor kind—for example, the *Vespasian Psalter* *ængel* and *drynctun*. The former is either an archaic spelling or a back-spelling; the latter probably indicates a minor Kentish influence. In Kent [y] had unrounded and lowered, merging with [ɛ], so that earlier *y* and *æ* were pronounced [ɛ]. Minor Kentish influence is not surprising in view of the close political ties between Mercia and Kent. The vowel remains unraised in the *Omont Leaf*, *gemẹng* and *mẹng*. It is important to notice that the further raisings of [æ] to [ɛ] / __ *r*, *l*, and *n* were all occurring in synchronic variation after the conditioning factor of i-umlaut had disappeared.

SMOOTHING

The discussion of breaking before *r*C was restricted to those environments in which the consonant of the cluster was not *c*, *g*, or *h*. The evidence from West Saxon indicates that breaking was more general: before any *r*C cluster or [χ], variously spelled *h*, *x*, *c*, *ch*, or *g*. The resultant diphthongization was masked in Anglian (Mercian *and* Northumbrian) Old English by the process of smoothing—loss of the glide element of the vowel cluster. The following

[11] Hilmer Ström, *Old English Personal Names in Bede's History* (Lund: Hakan Ohlsson, 1939), pp. 108–109.

135

data for the early texts show developments of West Germanic *a/
__C, rC (C = c, g, h).

There is considerable variety in the representation of the sound
before [χ] in the earliest glossaries:

	Epinal	Erfurt	Corpus
a		th[u]achl	slahae
ea	leactrocas	leactrocas	leactrogas
	leax		
æ	aex	aex (2X)	aex
	aectath	aechtath	aehtað
			braechtme
			*aexfaru
			*saex
			*blodsaex
			*þeohsaex
			*waexcondel
			*faexnis
			*laex
e	brectme	brectme	ðhuehl
		echtheri	
		lex	

The *Leyden Glossary* adds *blodsaex*. As the *Epinal, Erfurt*, and
Corpus Glossaries all agree on the vowel of *leactrocas*, it is reasonable
to assume that this was the form in their common archetype. This
would further indicate that the *æ* from the fronting of West Germanic
a broke to *ea* ([æə]) before it was smoothed back to *æ*. The vowel
of *Epinal leax* supports this claim, although the smoothing was
nearly complete by the time that the *Epinal* MS was written. The
independent glosses in *Corpus* (asterisked in the preceding listing)
indicate a completed sound change by A.D. 800. The *Omont Leaf*
has the same development as the *Corpus Glossary*, showing a
smoothed vowel in *nehterne* and *naehtnistig*. The smoothed vowel
may have been subject to raising, but the limited data are far from
conclusive. It is suggestive, however, that *Epinal* and *Erfurt* agree
(against *Corpus*) in *brectme*, especially since the further raising is

to be found in other texts of the peirod. The raising to *e* is found to the greatest extent in *Erfurt*, where *æ* from any source tends to be raised to a greater degree than in the other texts. The retracted vowel of *Erfurt th[u]achl* and *Corpus slahae* may, of course, be scribal errors, but they are better taken seriously in view of similar retractions in the *Vespasian Psalter*.

The *B. M. Cotton Tiberius C. ii* MS of Bede contains two different personal names with the element *Saex-*, spelled *Sex-* in the Northumbrian MSS. One name, Sexbald, does not occur in the Mercian text. The forms are:

Saexburg (2X)—wife of Eaconberct of Kent, later abbess of Ely,
     A.D. 680
Saexulfum (2X)—*Sexulfum, Saxulfum*—bishop of Mercia

Again the retracted vowel is found, but here, as in the following charter data, it may be due to confusion with the Latin *Saxonicum:*

700X715	(B-98)	*æhcha*
741	(B-160)	*suthsaxoniae*
764	(B-201)	*middelsaexum*
805X810	(B-330)	*ðaet weax*
831	(B-400)	*middelsaxanorum*

The document for A.D. 805X810 has Kentish connections and may reflect a Kentish influence. The *Codex Aureus* and the *Bede Glosses* each contain one example of the smoothed vowel: *almæhtiges*, and *mehte*, respectively. The glosses in *Royal 2.A.xx* contain occurrences both of the retracted and smoothed vowel: *almahtig, almahtigne, mæhtig, mæhtige, mæhtigan, næhte*. The *Martyrology* fragments, West Saxon copies of Mercian originals, contain only the broken vowel *ea*.

Smoothing is the rule in the *Vespasian Psalter*; the exceptions number less than 5%. The variation, however, follows the pattern of the texts listed above. There are three cases of a retracted vowel all occurring in *maht*—as in the Royal Glosses, although Luick treats these retractions as scribal errors.[12] Not only are they too regular to be so dismissed, they also anticipate similar retractions in the West Midland texts of the early Middle English and late Old English periods: *Chad—hlahendne, waxendum; Ancrene Wisse, Corpus Christi College Cambridge MS 402—lha(h)eð, lahhende; Bodleian MS 34—waxen.*

Examples for the environment __*r*C (C = *c, g, h*) are far more limited than those supplied immediately above. The early glossaries, however, provide sufficient information to establish the direction of the development at about A.D. 700–800.

	ea	*æ*	*e*
Epinal:	firstmearc	faerh	
	mearisern	maerh	
	we[a]rgrod		
	bearug		
Erfurt:		faerh	merisaen
		mærh	
		fristmaerc	
		waergrod	
Corpus:	fristmearc	waergrood	merg
	mearh	faerh	
	bearug	maerh	
		gemaercode	
		baercae	
		haerg	
		haerga	
		spærca	

The *Epinal* data again indicate that Primitive Old English **æ* broke to *ea* before being smoothed back to *æ*. Although the data are admittedly scant, it does appear that smoothing before [χ] was

[12] Karl Luick, *Historische Grammatik der Englischen Sprache* (Oxford: Basil Blackwell, 1964), pp. 190–196.

further developed (50%) than before *r*C (33%). Further raising is found in one of the five *Erfurt* glosses. Smoothing is also fairly regular in the *Corpus* MS, although three unsmoothed glosses give further testimony that a universal breaking precedes smoothing. The gloss *bearug*, shared by *Epinal* and *Corpus*, may show velar umlaut caused by the parasitic vowel. The forms may derive from the archetype, but it must be noted that the broken vowel also occurs in one of the only two possible cases of breaking in this environment to be found in the charters:

764 (B-201) *gumeninga hergae*
825 (B-384) *æt hearge*

The older charter shows the development which is typical for the *Vespasian Psalter*, in which all 13 glosses have *e: erc, gesnerc, hergas* (2X), *hergu(m* (2X), *merglice, wergcweodelade* (2X), *wergcweoðað, wer[g]cweoðende, wergcweodulnisse.*

West Germanic **a* in the smoothing environments could be subject to i-umlaut. Since the process of smoothing is to be seen as a synchronic force in the *Epinal Glossary* where i-umlaut is apparently complete, it follows that the effects of i-umlaut were completed by the period of smoothing. The data for *r*C have already been presented. The data for / __χi follow:

	æ	*e*
Epinal:	naect[h]raebn	ambechtae
	naecthraebn	steeli
		thuelan
		ambect
		nectaegalae
		nectigalae
Erfurt:	ambaet	ambechtae
	hæ,ctæ,gela	steli
		thuelan
		necegle
		nect-
		nethhræbn

4 Conspiracy and Competition in the Implementation of Change

The reflex of West Germanic *a/ __χi in the *Epinal* and *Erfurt Glossaries* accords well with the data for the i-umlaut of Germanic *a in general breaking position. That is, e prevails, and there are no residual forms to support an intermediate state in which there was a glide formation (to [æa]) before i-umlaut took place. The residue, in fact, attests an intermediate stage of [æ] followed by raising to [ɛ]. It is entirely possible that the conditioning factor for i-umlaut blocked the breaking process but encouraged the raising of the unbroken vowel. The data from the *Corpus Glossary*, however, depart dramatically from the *Epinal–Erfurt* material.

	æ	e
Corpus:	ambaect	oembecht
	naectegale	steli
	naeht-	thuelan
	naectgenge	nehtęgale
	naectegale	
	staeli	
	gesca slaet	
	ðuaelum	

The further raised e is found in *Corpus* only in those glosses which are common to *Epinal* and *Erfurt*. The examples split between æ and e in the *Omont Leaf: ecid* and *ece* but *-ęcz* (2X). In the six glosses peculiar to *Corpus*, only æ is found. In other words, i-umlaut appears only to have taken place in the glosses derived from the archetype. I-umlaut was a productive process in the phonology of the archetype, but was never completed as is evidenced by the variation in the early texts. Alternation deriving from the variable application of i-umlaut to an underlying /æ/ must have continued until the period in which the conditioning factor was lost. At that point, underlying /æ/ was reinterpreted in terms of the synchronic smoothing before [χ]. This is the situation for the scribe of the *Corpus Glossary*.

THE RAISING OF [æ]

As it has been noted in the earlier sections of this chapter, there was a strong general tendency in the earliest glossaries to raise the [æ] which had been fronted from West Germanic *a*. The tendency was strong enough to compete with other conditioned developments of [æ]. In what follows, these raisings are summarized and are given in descending order of frequency. The developments in items (1), (4), and (5), of course, are common to all Old English dialects; (3) is a general Anglian change; (8) anticipates a late Old English, early Middle English development; (7) appears frequently in late Old Northumbrian texts.

		Percentage *e*			
	Epinal	*Erfurt*	*Corpus*	*Leyden*	*VP*
(1) *a/ __Ci*	all	all	all	all	all
(2) *a/ __lli*	all	all	all	all	none
(3) *a/ __rCi*	77	84	80	—	all
(4) *a/ __Ni*	25	66	90	all	all
(5) *a/ __i*	66	77	40	—	0
(6) *a/ __*	20	50	8	—	0
(7) *a/ __rC*	0	20	0	—	0
C = *c, g, h*				—	
(8) *a/ __lCi*	0	28	5	—	0
(9) *a/ __rC*	0	22	3	24	0

The raising of the *æ*s produced from several umlaut processes formed an early Mercian phonological conspiracy, the effect of which was an extended general tendency to raise [æ] to [ɛ]. It began early and was evident in *Epinal* and further developed in *Erfurt*, where it was even extended to the various smoothing products. The linguistic developments take a sharp turn in the language of the *Corpus Glossary*. There the general tendency is restricted and smoothing environments excluded.

141

4 Conspiracy and Competition in the Implementation of Change

THE "SECOND FRONTING"

At the same time that the raising of [æ] in the above conditioned changes was being specialized and proceeding toward completion, the raising was extended to environments in which no intervening sound changes competed. That is, [æ] from any source participated in the conspiracy to raise. The culmination of the conspiracy was the language of the *Vespasian Psalter*, in which *œ* from any source other than smoothing is raised to *e*. The following is a summary of the data for the unconditioned raising—the so-called second fronting of [æ]:

	Epinal	*Erfurt*	*Corpus*
œ	58	51	158
e	15	33	22
a	2	6	0

The raised vowels represent a substantial portion of the lexicon in each of the early texts. To represent the fronting in terms of percentages (20, 37, and 30 respectively) is, however, misleading. The fronted forms are not uniformly distributed throughout the lexicon. Almost all of the *e*s occur before developments of the Germanic voiced bilabial fricative which was variously represented in the earliest texts as *b, f,* and *p*. As *Erfurt* alone supplies a significant number of examples in environments other than / __β, only data for the sensitive environment will be reproduced here.[13]

	œ	*e*
Epinal:	*hraebrebletae*	*lerb*
	hraebnę	*lebil*
	[h]raebn	*lebil*
	staeblidrae	*cefr*

[13] The remaining examples can be found in Chadwick, "Studies," pp. 190–196.

The "Second Fronting"

æ	e
staebplegan	cebertuun
araebndae	teblae
r[a]ebsid	tebelstan
raeped	teblith
edscaept	teblere
scaeptloan	reftras
waeffsas	sceptloum
saeppae	
anhaebd	

Erfurt:

æ	e
araebndae	hebre-
hraebn	nefern
hræfnæs	lebrae
nethræbn	lebil
hraebn	steblidrae
scæbplegan	cefr
caeber	arepsit
endestẹb	repsitwaes
edscaept	refset
uaeps	tefil
sẹpae	tebilstan
anhaefd	teblith
laepaeuincæ	teblere
	lebil
	lebil
	lebrae
	tebleri
	reftras
	sceptloum

Corpus:

æ	e
haeb	heber
haebrn	lebr
haebern	leber
araef[n]de	lebil
araefndum	lebl
hraefn	lebel
hraefnes	cefer
hraefnaes	ceber
hraefn	uunydecreft

143

æ	e
scraeb	tebl
staeflíðre	teblstan
staebplagan	tebleth
waefs	teblere
uuaefsas	reftras
ahaefd	sceploum
waefs	sceptog
caebr	etspe (for sepe)
caefli	lepeuuince
caebestr	
raefsit-	
endistaeb	
fraefeli	
fraefeleo	
edscaeft	
scaeptloan	

These data summarized are:

	Epinal	Erfurt	Corpus
æ	13	14	26
e	11	19	18
Percentage es	44	57	40

Second fronting began as a variable rule sensitive to only a very restricted environment. The balance of raised æs in other environments is sporadic: *Epinal* 3/51; *Erfurt* 9/52; *Corpus*, 4/133. It is because the raised æs in environments in which other sound changes intervene are found in such higher magnitude that the second fronting is here considered part of the conspiracy to raise rather than the motivating force in the general tendency to raise. The environment for raising in *Erfurt* has begun to spread; / __st causes raising in three of four instances: *mestum, best, festis, festinnum*. Phonetic environment is not the only force operating in the glosses that show raising. Many of the words in which the raising is most frequent are loan words: *lebr, lebil, cefr, teblae*, etc. That is, the sound

144

change is advancing at a faster rate through this subset of the lexicon.

The several forms of *baeso* and *maettoc* present problems of their own. In particular, how is the *eo* spelling to be explained?

> *Epinal: baeso, bru[u]nbesu, mettocas, mettocas, mettocas, maettoc*
> *Erfurt: beoso, brunbesu, mettocas, metocas, metticas, mettoc*
> *Corpus: beosu, beosu, meottucas, mettocas, meottoc*

First, it must be borne in mind that there is considerable confusion in the earliest texts between *eo* and *ea* ([æə]). These spellings might, then, represent mere orthographic variation in the representation of the [æə] diphthong. However, the undiphthongized vowel is often written *e*—the /æ/ has undergone second fronting. These *eo* spellings, then, probably represent the further velar umlaut of the raised vowel.

There is further evidence of an important nature for the second fronting. Several hypercorrections are to be found. First, there are several cases in which West Germanic *e* is spelled *æ:*

> *Epinal: uuaegn, uuaegbradae, hlaeodrindi*
> *Erfurt: cæle, aebordrotae, saegaesetu*
> *Corpus: caeli, saes*

In addition, *Erfurt* has three glosses in which the i-umlaut of fronted *æ* (from West Germanic *a*) is spelled *æ* (*eordraestae, caebis, uuęb*); *Corpus* has six (*staege, waech, asaecgan, waebtaeg, wraeccan, suaeðila*). These may be residue from the incomplete raising caused by i-umlaut.

While the glossaries offer early data for the second fronting, the charters offer a cross section of the Mercian speech community over an extended period of time. Before proceeding with a presentation of the data from the Mercian official documents, one should note that the environment in which the second fronting apparently began is missing in these early charters. Examples of a

145

second fronting, then, will signal a generalization of the conditioning environment:

		æ	*e*
697	(B-97)	*aethilburgae*	
		aedilburgae	
736	(B-154)	*aethilbalt*	*edilbalt*
		aetdilbalt	
		aethilbaldo	
		ęthilbaldi	
		aethilric	
*742	(B-162)	*æðelbald-* (4X)	*huetlac*
		æðelberht	
		æðelfrið	
759	(B-187)	*æt*	
767	(B-176)	*aethelnothes*	
770	(B-203)	*æðelmundo*	
		æðelbaldi	
779	(B-230)	*æt*	
788	(B-254)	*aethilmod*	
*793X796	(B-274)	*æðelmund-* (2X)	
		æðelheardi	
*798	(B-289)	*æðelhard*	
		æðelmundi	
		æt (2X)	
		ðeræt	
799	(B-293)	*aeðilhard*	
		aeðilheard	
		aethelmund	
801	(B-301)	*aethelbald*	
		æðelmund	
		æthelheardu[s]	
*803	(B-310)	*æðelheard-* (3X)	
		æt	
803	(B-312)	*aeðelheardus* (2X)	
		aeþelheah	
		aeþelhæh	
		aeþelhelm	

The "Second Fronting"

		æ	*e*
		dæghelm (2X)[14]	
805	(B-319)	*aedilheard* (2X)	
		aet	
*805	(B-321)	*aeðelheard* (2X)	
		aeðilgeard	
*805X807	(B-318)	*æðelnoð-* (3X)	*hweðer*
		æðelierd	
		æðelhun- (2X)	
		mæsseprioste (2X)	
		ðæt (3X)	
*805X810	(B-330)	*huaeder*	*gehueder*
		ðæt (10X)	*messan*
		æt (6X)	*ðet*
		ðætte (2X)	*aelmessan* (4X)
		mæge (2X)	*ðette*
		-dæg	*festendæg*
		dæges	
		fuguldaeg	
		ðeræt	
		Back-spellings: *gæfe* (3X), *forcuæ,denan, forecuaedenan*	
*811	(B-332)	*ðæt* (2X)	*et*
		æt (5X)	
		aeðelheard (2X)	
		aeðelhun	
		aeðelhear	
*811	(B-335)	*ðæt*	
		aet	
		aeðeluulf (2X)	
		aelfþyrð	
		aeðelhear	

[14] Dæghelm signs under Eadwulf, Bishop of Sydnaceaster. He was probably from Lindsay.

		æ	*e*
811	(B-339)	*aeðelwulf*	*hrofescester*
		aeðelheah	
*812	(B-341)	*æt* (2X)	
		aet	
		aeðelheardi	
		aedelheah	
814	(B-343)	*aelfðyrða*	*ðet*
		æðelnoð	*ðem*
		æðelheah	
		æðelmund	
*814	(B-348)	*æt*	
		ælfþyrþ	
*822	(B-370)	*fæstingmenn*	
		ędelwald	
*823	(B-374)	*æðelwald*	
*824	(B-378)	*aeðelhun*	
		aeðelwald	
		æt (3X)	
		ðæt	
*825	(B-384)	*aet* (2X)	
		æt (13X)	
		aeðelwald	
		aelfgyð (2X)	
		dægmund	
*825X832	(B-380)	*æt*	
		aeðeluulfo	
		aeðelhun	
		daegmund	
*831	(B-400)	*aeðelhard*	
836	(B-416)	*ðæs* (3X)	
		wæs (2X)	
		æþelhard	
		æþeluulf	
		ælfstan	
		fæstingmenn	

		æ	e
		cræft	
		æt (7X)	
		ðæt	
844X5	(B-452)	*æðelwulf*	
		ælfstan	
		ðæs (2X)	
		fæstna	
		mæge	
		daeg	
		ðeræt	
		æt	
		ðæt	
*873	(B-536)	*ẹt* (2X)	*et*
		þẹs	*ðes*
		soðfẹstlice	*elmessan*
		fẹstnie	*ðet*
		ðẹt (3X)	*þet* (2X)
		þẹt (3X)	*dege* (2X)
		ẹfter (5X)	
		mẹge (2X)	
		dẹge (2X)	
		dẹg (3X)	
		fẹdrenmega	
		rehtfẹderen	

Most of the data are limited to personal names (with *æðel-*) and words that do not get full stress (*æt*, which retains that form even in the *Vespasian Psalter*, etc.). However, as Kuhn has pointed out, and as is evident from the data of this study, the second fronting is a relatively late change.[15] The sound change, variable in the language of the Mercians, would naturally have less effect on non-Mercians than would a completed sound change, like the nasal development of *a*. The charter data, taking these factors into con-

[15] Sherman M. Kuhn, "The Dialect of the Corpus Glossary," *PMLA* 54 (1939): 16.

sideration, do attest considerable Mercian influence, especially after A.D. 800. For example, [æ] and [ɛ] have completely fallen together in the language of the scribe of B-330.

The Kentish and Kentish–Mercian charters provide interesting data for the development of the second fronting in Kent:

679 (B-45)	*aedilmaeri*
732 (B-148)	*aethilberht-* (3X)
	aehiliaerdi
741 (B-160)	*aethilberht-* (2X)
	aeðelhuni
	aethelnothi

Notice that second fronting and Mercian letter forms are absent from the Kentish charters that antedate the rise of Mercian domination of Kent. The following six charters are documents with Kentish connections that were written during the apex of Mercian influence. (As the full data have already been given, only summary counts of forms will be repeated here.)

		æ	*e*
803	(B-312)	7	0
*805X807	(B-318)	18	1
*805X810	(B-330)	35	10 (5 back-spellings)
*811	(B-332)	11	1
*824	(B-378)	8	0
825X832	(B-380)	4	0

The charters covering the period of the decay of Mercian authority show a marked increase in the occurrence of second fronting:

	æ	*e*
*833X839 (B-412)	*æt*	*et* (2X)
	æfter (3X)	*efter*
	ðæt (4X)	*festnie* (2X)
	ðæt (2X)	*dege*
	þæt (4X)	*deg* (2X)

The "Second Fronting"

		_æ_	_e_
		dæge	_hebbe_ (2X)
		hwæder	
		maege	
		ðeræt	
		alles hwæt (2X)	
		hæbbe	
*843	(B-405)	_æðelmund_	_wes_
		ðęt	_et_
			hebbe
			festnie
			deimund
845	(B-417)	_æfter_ (2X)	_efter_
		_æt_	_et_
			ælmeslic
			ðes
			dege
			dei (5X)
			liffest
			befestan
			festnie
			eðelwulf
			eðelred
850	(B-403)		_scel_
			elmesse
			_et_ (4X)
			δ_em_
			hwet
			dei
			ðet (2X)
			ðes
			sunnandeg
			hebbe
859	(B-497)		_et_
			deimund
			ðet
			eðelmode (2X)
			eðelwulf

151

		æ	*e*
			eðelbeald
			eðeric
			eð[el]noð
863	(B-405)	*ðæm*	*ðem*
			ðet (2X)
			gefestnie
			elmessan
			hebbe (2X)
868	(B-519)	*ęðelmund* (2X)	*eðelweald* (3X)
		ęðelwulf	*eðeredes*
		eðelred	*deibearht*
*867X870	(B-404)		*elmestlicust*
			eðelwald
			eðelmodes
			elfstan
			ðet (4X)
			were
			wes
			eðelnoð
			dege
			hwelc
			ðes (2X)
			ðet (2X)
			festnie
			et
			hebbe
			yfter[16]

These data would indicate that the Kentish were at first slow to learn the second fronting from the politically dominant Mercians, but then quickly imitated the speech of their masters and fully extended the raising to any *æ*s from all sources.

In the remaining texts of this study, the raising of *æ* from West Germanic **a* is found as the rule in the *Vespasian Psalter*, the *Lorica Prayer*, and the glosses to *Royal 2.A.20*. As the *Vespasian*

[16] The *y* here is a Kentish hypercorrection signaling the falling together of Kentish *e* and *y*.

Psalter is virtually without exception, a full recitation of the raised forms would be pointless. The exceptions are usually found in words that are generally not fully stressed and in strong verbs:

cwaeð, cwæð (2X)
ett, deg, mægne, fet (all probably scribal errors)
ðæt (151X), *ðætte* (2X), *ðaet* (2X), *ðaette, þæt, þætte*
*æt:et::*19:1
ðæt (225X), *ðet* (25X)

The *Lorica Prayer* contains one word with Germanic **a*, and it shows fronting—*deg*. The *Royal Glosses* have *ber, cweþ* (9X), *deg-* (3X), *deghweamlice, et* (2X); *eteaw, etfest, feder* (3X)—but also *fædor, fædrum, federum, festenne, sigerfestnisse, megden, megne, nesðyrlum, wes* (5X), *weter, þes, ðes* (2X), *þet* (4X). One of two glosses in the *Blickling Psalter* (*geheplicnissum*) contains the fronted vowel. Only sporadic examples are to be found in the balance of the texts: the Mercian *Bede* (*lestinga he, uetlingua caester, uinued*), one scratched gloss to *Bede* (*hern*, with an excrescent *h*, metathesis, no breaking, then raising). The vowel is never raised in the *Omont Leaf*, but that text belongs to the period of decay of Mercian authority.

THE VELAR UMLAUT OF [æ]

Another sound change affects the vowel developed from Germanic **a*. West Germanic **a*, which was not fronted before back vowels (or was fronted and then retracted), undergoes a fronting in several early Mercian texts. The fronted *æ* is itself rarely found. The newly developed sound is most often immediately diphthongized (by velar umlaut) to [æə], spelled *ea*. The earliest glossaries show the beginnings of this sound change and its extension:

	Epinal	*Erfurt*	*Corpus*
a	28	29	58
æ	6	6	7
ea	7	7	20

4 Conspiracy and Competition in the Implementation of Change

The following table includes all examples of fronting (and the subsequent velar umlaut where applicable):

	Epinal	Erfurt	Corpus
Percentage fronting	25	25	32
æ	gaebuli	haera	spaeca
	baeso	uualhaebuc	naec[ad]
	haeguthorn	staefad	asclaecadun
	stęgu	slaegu	rægu
	claedur	maefuldur	hlaegulendi
			slaegu
ea	heamol	sceadae	heagoðorn
	bearug	sceaba	reagufinc
	scead[u]	hreadamus	heagaspen
	hreathamus	hreathmus	weagat
	hreadaemus	healful (for heamul)	onseacan
	uuicingsceadan		onseacan
	sceaba		geaduling (2X)
			geuueada
			cleadur
			geabuli (3X)
			geabulismonung
			heamul
			bearug[17]
			aexfearu
			sceadu
			sceadan
			sceaba

The relationship between fronting and velar umlaut in the *Epinal* and *Erfurt Glossaries* can be expressed by the feeding ordering of the following two variable rules:

[17] This form (from *bærg) may show either breaking or velar umlaut via the epenthetic vowel.

The Velar Umlaut of [æ]

(A) a → ⟨æ⟩ / __⟨CV$_{+back}$ .32⟩

(B) ∅ → ⟨a⟩ / æ __⟨CV$_{+back}$ .50⟩

Recalling that smoothing is complete in the *Corpus Glossary* before [χ], the data for the application of the fronting and velar umlaut rules are interesting. The segment *æ* undergoes velar umlaut categorically except when in a smoothing environment, where velar umlaut is variable. These generalizations may profitably be restated:

(A) a → ⟨æ⟩ / __ ⟨CV$_{+back}$ .32⟩

(B) ∅ → ⟨ə⟩ / æ __ $\left\langle \begin{matrix} *CV_{+back} \\ =CV_{+back} \end{matrix} .50 \right\rangle$

The *Vespasian Psalter* is the lineal descendant of the glossaries. The fronting is complete:

(A) a → æ / __ CV$_{+back}$

Glide formation is categorical except before *c*, *g*, and *h*:

(B) ∅ → ə / æ __ CV$_{+back}$

Rule (A) feeds (B) and has become crucially ordered before it. In the chronological development from *Epinal* to the *Vespasian Psalter*, fronting has developed from a variable rule to a completed sound change. Velar umlaut has progressed from a nonconditioned variable rule to a variably conditioned sound change and finally to a completed sound change in which the variable constraint has become categorical. The smoothing environment precludes raising (by second fronting) and subsequent velar umlaut. The rules account for the forms *dægas*, *dræca*, etc. (from the *Vespasian Psalter*).

As in the case of raising, the fronting is not universal in the Mercian texts, but examples of velar umlaut of fronted **a* (that is, *æ*) are to be found scattered through the texts of this study: the Mercian *Bede* (*peadda*—the name of a Mercian; *beaduðegn*—the other MSS have *bada-*) and the *Lorica Glosses* (*heagospianu(m*,

155

lundleogan, lunleogu(m—the last two from **-laga,* and showing the confusion of *eo* and *ea*). The *Omont Leaf* shows the fronting and subsequent velar umlaut in one gloss, *eapul.* Forms are also common in the charters:

759	(B-187)	*headda*
*793X799	(B-274)	*eafing* (from **eafaing*)
801	(B-201)	*haeðoberht*
803	(B-312)	*heaðored*
*805X810	(B-330)	*ðeara*
*811	(B-332)	*reacoluensae*
*822	(B-370)	*beadhard* (from *beadu-*)
*823	(B-374)	*beadhard*
*825	(B-384)	*þeara*
825X832	(B-380)	*ðeara*
*831	(B-400)	*headda*

Most of the charters with the velar umlaut product *ea* also have Mercian letter forms. The development of *ea* is also known in the Kentish and Kentish–Mercian charters of the period. Campbell makes this observation[18] but fails to take Kent's troubled political history into account. Of the forms he cites, the earliest examples are all found in documents that also contain Mercian letter forms.

DRESHER'S ACCOUNT OF THE SECOND FRONTING

B. Elan Dresher recently proposed a new interpretation of the vowel allophony of Old English /æ/.[19] His analysis begins with the

[18] A. Campbell, "An Old English Will," *JEGP* 37 (1938): 148.
[19] Bezalel Elan Dresher, "The Mercian Second Fronting: A Case of Rule Loss in Old English," *Linguistic Inquiry* 11 (1980): 47–73, and "Second Fronting in the Old English Dialect of the Omont Leaf," paper presented at the Annual Meeting of the Linguistic Society of America, 1981.

Dresher's Account of the Second Fronting

traditional assumption (stated in generative terms) that underlying Germanic /a/ became underlying Old English /æ/. He continues by making the sensible suggestion that retraction of /æ/ is really two separate phenomena: (*a*) the process by which /æ/ is backed to /a/ before *l*C—retraction; and (*b*) the process by which /æ/ is backed to /a/ before back vowels—*a*-restoration. The distinction makes a difference when we consider the complex of changes that have gone under the single label "second fronting" in traditional studies. Dresher continues to follow the traditional view that *æ* became *e* through the addition of a rule of *æ*-raising. But instead of following the traditional analysis which relates the fronting of *a* to *æ* by adding a fronting rule, he posits that one can generate the expected surface forms as a result of the loss of his rule of *a*-restoration. The underlying /æ/ would then be subject to velar umlaut. By separating out the various phenomena, Dresher can convincingly and economically explain the variety of forms that are possible with the Mercian dialects:

1. The *Epinal Glossary*, the *Erfurt Glossary*, and the *Corpus Glossary*, which have a variable raising rule and are in the process of losing the *a*-restoration rule
2. The *Vespasian Psalter*, for which both the addition of the raising rule and the loss of the *a*-restoration rule are categorical
3. The *Royal Glosses*, which have the raising rule but have not lost *a*-restoration
4. The *Omont Leaf*, which does not have the raising rule but has lost *a*-restoration

Some sample derivations adding a variationist's perspective to Dresher's work will clarify the process.

The *Corpus Glossary* data exhibit the following three interactions of the variable rules:

With retraction, *a*-restoration, and a variable second fronting raising:

Underlying	/æld/	/fæt/	/fæt + u/	/wer + as/
Retraction	ald	—	—	—

157

a-restoration	—	—	fat + u	—
⟨Second fronting⟩	—	⟨fet ~ fæt⟩	—	—
Orthographic	ald	fet ~ fæt	fatu	weras

With the addition of a variable velar umlaut:

Underlying	/fæt + u/	/wer + as/
a-restoration	fat + u	—
⟨Velar umlaut⟩		⟨weər + as ~ wer + as⟩
Orthographic	fatu	weoras ~ weras

With a-restoration variable:

Underlying	/fæt + u/
⟨a-restoration⟩	⟨fat + u ~ fæt + u⟩
Velar umlaut	⟨fat + u ~ fæət + u⟩
Orthographic	fatu ~ featu

In the *Vespasian Psalter*, we find retraction, the raising (called second fronting), and velar umlaut all in categorical operation, but *a*-restoration lost:

Underlying	/æld/	/fæt/	/fæt + u/	/wer + as/
Retraction	ald	—	—	—
Second fronting	—	fet	—	—
Velar umlaut	—	—	fæət + u	weər + as
Orthographic	ald	fet	featu	weoras

In the language of the *Omont Leaf*, retraction and velar umlaut operate, but *a*-restoration has been lost and *æ*-raising has not been added to the grammar:

Underlying	/cælde/	/bæð/	/æpul/	/belon + an/
Retraction	calde	—	—	—
Velar umlaut	—	—	æəpul	beəlon + an
Orthographic	calde	bæð	eapul	beolonan

Even though I find Dresher's arguments plausible and an improvement on the traditional analysis, I have maintained the traditional approach in the body of my discussion of these changes. I did so in order for my interpretation to be readily accessible to traditionalists. Further, Dresher's most convincing argument (from the *Omont Leaf*) hinges upon a single example from a text of questionable date and origin. If future discoveries are made of texts from this period, I fully expect them to corroborate Dresher's analysis.

CONSPIRACY AND COMPETITION

The data of the previous chapter dealt with a single sound changing as a response to a single phonetic environment. As a result, the patterns of variation emerged in startling relief. This chapter, on the other hand, dealt with several sets of highly complex interrelationships. Even though the patterns of variation are less immediately obvious, they are clear patterns nonetheless. The segment [æ] was highly volatile, as it had been earlier and would prove to be again in the history of the language. The sound that had been readily retracted, or had resisted fronting, again exhibited a sensitivity to the influence of [+back] segments—back consonants in breaking, back vowels in velar umlaut. The resultant diphthongal allophones began variably, and only in the course of time—and not in all varieties—did they achieve the status of categorically predictable alternations.

Several different environments (the high, front umlauting vowel, the consonants palatalized by the umlauting vowel, the nasals when further influenced by an umlauting vowel) contributed to the raising of the unstable [æ]. They had a combinative effect in Mercian-dominated communities. There was either a more generalized tendency to raise [æ] in the West Midlands (where the sound change continued into Middle English times) which diffused irregularly via political influence, or the general conspiracy to raise became associated with the speech ways of the dominant Mercians. At any rate, an increased tendency to raise [æ], conditioned or unconditioned, was a concomitant of Mercian political ascendancy. In fact, the data from the charters would indicate that the Kentish second fronting

159

(raising of [æ]) began during the period when Mercia completely dominated Kent.

These data include several cases of sound changes in competition with each other: [æ] raises or forms a centralizing off-glide, /a/ is fronted only to be diphthongized. With second fronting and *a*-restoration we have interesting examples of sound changes that did not succeed as widely implemented developments. The data suggest that competition among changes seriously inhibits progress toward completion.

5

VARIATION AND
CHANGE IN
MERCIAN OLD ENGLISH

ATA like that offered in the previous two chapters attest to a series of sound changes that occurred in Old English during the period of the first written texts. The progress of those changes can be seen in patterns of variation which record innovations beginning irregularly in small lexical and phonological subsets of the language and then spreading with increasing regularity to the status of allophonic alternations. As those data deal only with the developments of one West Germanic sound, they are perhaps an insufficient basis from which to generalize about our ability to study sound change in progress by means of manuscript data. This chapter provides the wide range of data which is necessary to demonstrate that the variable manuscript data of the first English texts reflect structured heterogeneity rather than the random variation of scribal whim. The frequency of these variations also develops chronologically toward the allophony of well-attested, completed sound changes. Variation in individual texts may at first seem unsystematic, but the collective pattern argues for a dynamic perspective of ongoing change.

PREHISTORIC OLD ENGLISH /$\bar{æ}$/

Old English /$\bar{æ}$/ developed from a variety of sources which are easily confused. Chadwick's notational device—$\bar{æ}^1$, $\bar{æ}^2$, $\bar{æ}^3$, $\bar{æ}^4$—is useful in keeping the etymological values separate in general discussions:

1. West Germanic *$\bar{a}$ (Germanic *$\bar{æ}$)[1] was fronted to $\bar{æ}$[1]. Although this sound was regularly written *e* in many varieties of Old English, the usual West Saxon spelling *æ* (and a variable residue of *æ* forms in early texts) points to an intermediate stage of [æ:] for general Old English.
2. Germanic *ai developed to Primitive Old English *$\bar{a}$ which in turn could be i-umlauted to $\bar{æ}$[2], spelled *æ* except in Kentish texts where *e* spellings indicate a subsequent raising.
3. The sound represented by $\bar{æ}$[3] developed from the i-umlaut of $\bar{æ}a$ (from Germanic *au); $\bar{æ}$[4] was the normal smoothing product of $\bar{æ}a$.

As each of these sounds was represented variably in early Old English spelling, they warrant being considered in some detail.

GERMANIC *$\bar{æ}$

Primitive Old English *$\bar{æ}$ from Germanic $\bar{æ}$ was usually raised to [e], variously written *e, ei,* or *ee* in the earliest glossaries:[2]

Epinal: *setungae, gerlicae, megsibbi, strelbora, beer, resung,*
grei, geberu, thys geri, gredig, redboran,
threatmelum, ormetum, mere uueard, leceas,
styccimelu(m leciuuyrt, heringas, bledrae, uuemotan,
hraebrebletae, t[h]res, thres, bredipannae, meeg,

---

[1] Some scholars have claimed that as Germanic *$\bar{æ}$ was not in contrast with a short *$æ$ it ought not be labeled a long vowel. However, the sound developed into a long vowel in Old English, Gothic ($\bar{e}$), Old Saxon ($\bar{a}$), Old Frisian ($\bar{e}$), Old High German ($\bar{a}$), Old Icelandic ($\bar{o}$), etc. Unless one assumes that each of these languages developed a long sound independently, it seems best to mark Germanic *$æ$ long even though it had no short counterpart.

[2] Chadwick, "Studies," pp. 256–270.

> *strel, colþred, birednae, blestbaelg, ethm,*[3] *bredisern,*
> *blec, blechta*

Erfurt: *setungae, gernlicae, megsibbi, strelbora, beer,*
resung, grei, geberu, thysgeri, gredig, redboran,
threatmelum, ormetum, mereuuard, leceas,
scyccimelu(m, leciuyrt, heringas, bledrae, unemo,
hebrebletae, thres, ðres, breitibannæ, fotmelum, bled,
nep, nedlæ, oeghuuer, sp(re)ici, blest, gregos,
lenlibreda, beel, blec-, blectha

Corpus: *setunge, gerlice, meg-, strel-, beer, resung, grei,*
geberu, -gere, gredig, red-, melum, ormetum, mere-,
leceas, melum, leci, heringas, bledre, uue[me]tta,
-blete, ðres, brediponne, meig, stregl, -nethle-,
oeghuer, -speci, -ðred, birednae, netl, ebnwege,
gredge, el, healecas, bletid, fer, iserngrei, ðred, cese,
gebero, grei, wearn melum, þys gere, feringa,
feringe, frioletan, frioleta, hebelðred, lendebrede,
geuueted, mece risigan, megcualm, styccimelum,
weðl, her, heðir, resunge, edmelu, strel, gierende,
frioleta, gebreded, gebero, deid, greig, eil, blechta,
bleci

Leyden: beel, dredum, [friu]lactum (probably for *-laetum*)

The presence of the i-umlauting vowel may have been a factor in hastening the raising to *e* (*Epinal mere, leceas, leciuuyrt,* etc., for example), but one must not confuse $\bar{æ}^1$ from Germanic $*\bar{æ}$ with $\bar{æ}^2$ from the i-umlaut of Germanic $*ai$. Pheifer,[4] ignoring the sound work of Chadwick[5] and Dieter,[6] includes such glosses as *obaerstaelid*

---

[3] The original *e-t* ligature in this gloss is ambiguously "corrected" by a later hand to something which Sweet read as [*d*]*et* and Schlutter read as [*a*]*et*. It is certainly not a standard *æ-t* as Pheifer reports in his edition. I follow the first scribe's original reading, although the *Corpus* reading *aethm* indicates that the "correction" as Schlutter read it may have been the reading in the archetype.

[4] J. D. Pheifer, *Old English Glosses in the Epinal–Erfurt Glossary* (Oxford: Oxford University Press), p. lx.

[5] Chadwick, "Studies," pp. 210–212.

[6] Ferdinand Dieter, *Ueber Sprache und Mundart der ältesten englischen Denkmäler* (Göttingen: G. Calvör, 1885), p. 17.

and *raedinnae* in his list of words containing Germanic *ǣ (ǣ¹) and thus unnecessarily exaggerates both the rate of occurrence of ǣ in the archetype and the Anglo-Saxon confusion of [ǣ] and [ē] as an influence in the phonology of the glossaries. These and similar examples are best treated as ǣ², the i-umlaut of Germanic *ai*. On the other hand, it is difficult to understand Pheifer's motivation in treating the doubtful *blec-* forms as exceptional raisings of i-umlauted Old English ā and hence a potential Kentish influence or Anglian raising before palatal and dental consonants.[7] I have treated them as nonexceptional—among the ordinary developments of ǣ¹.[8] Although it is necessary to observe and attempt to explain variation in the early texts, it is certainly unproductive to generate variation.

The glossaries do, however, have some examples of Germanic *ǣ spelled *æ:*

Epinal	Erfurt	Corpus
blaeed		blẹd
naep		naep
mið naeðlae	draed	blaesbaeg
oghuuaer	biraednae	aethm
felospraeci		blaec-

The agreement of *Epinal* and *Corpus* on the two *æ* spellings may point to the existence of such forms in the archetype. As all three texts never agree, these forms must have been rare even in the archetype. That is, the sound change was complete or near complete by about A.D. 700. The *Bede Glosses* give four examples with *e* (*erendwrica, nedran, strelas, godwrecnissum*) against one gloss with *æ* (*gehwaer*). Germanic ǣ is raised in the *Omont Leaf: aslepnum, let, scepes, weat, lecedom,* and *lecnige.*

This general state of affairs is also seen in the names in the early MSS of Bede's *History: Reduald, Suefred, Eumer, Eanfled.* There are, however, important variants. *Red-* appears once (out of 12 occurrences) in the Moore Bede as *Raed-;* three times, in the Mercian

---

[7] Pheifer, *Epinal–Erfurt,* p. lxviii.
[8] As does Chadwick, "Studies," p. 210n.

Bede. *Suæbhard* occurs once in each. Ström correctly notes that Raedrid was a prefect in Kent and Suæbhard was a king of Kent where $\bar{æ}$ and $\bar{e}$ from any source were widely confused.[9] So great was this confusion in Kent that the charter data for $\bar{æ}^1$ (Germanic $*\bar{æ}$) and $*\bar{æ}^2$ (the i-umlaut of Primitive Old English $*\bar{a}$) can most profitably be discussed together. Otherwise, $\bar{e}$ was a general Mercian development of Germanic $*\bar{æ}$; the exceptions, too infrequent to be linguistically significant, are found in the texts that are late West Saxon copies of Mercian originals.

THE i-UMLAUT OF PRIMITIVE OLD ENGLISH *a

The textual representations of this sound are important to this study because of its later Kentish development to [ē]. There is no evidence for any such early Mercian raising. The *Epinal Glossary* has only *æ* (26 examples spelled with *æ* or *ę*). Most of the same glosses are to be found in *Corpus*, also spelled with graphic variants of *æ*. The confusion in the *Erfurt Glossary* of /$\bar{æ}$/ and /$\breve{e}$/ from any source has already been noted; so it is not surprising to find *e* in nine of the glosses common to the early glossaries.[10] The complete correspondence between *Epinal* and *Corpus* attests *æ* forms in the archetype. In 4 examples (out of 39), *Corpus* has an *e* in glosses not common to the *Erfurt–Epinal* material. These glosses (*to gelestunne, scultheta, uuegið, stictenel*) must be viewed in their relationship to developments in other texts, especially the charters in which the alternations are the most pronounced.

We have already noted in this study that Anglo-Saxon linguistic heterogeneity is nowhere more evident than in the charters. Consider the following data for $\bar{æ}^1$ and $\bar{æ}^2$ as found in documents having Kentish connections. As usual, the presence of Mercian letter forms is marked with an asterisk:

[9] Hilmer Ström, *Old English Personal Names in Bede's History* (Lund: Hakan Ohlsson, 1939).

[10] The full data may be found in Chadwick, "Studies," pp. 210–212.

The i-Umlaut of Primitive Old English *a

	$\overline{æ}^1$		$\overline{æ}^2$	
	æ	e	æ	e
700 (B-98)		stretleg		
*805X832 (B-318)	suæ (2X)	were	aræddan	
		sprece	æhte (2X)	
			bæm	
			gedæle	
			nænig	
			ðæm	
*805X810 (B-330)	ðær (3X)	red	ðære (2X)	arede
	wæron	suesendum (2X)	æghwilc (3X)	hele
	swæ (6X)		ðæm (2X)	ðere (4X)
	aecan		mæst	clendra
	uuęge		tuęgen	gedele
	suęsendum		huaetendra	ðem (2X)
*811 (B-332)		magonsetum		
845X853 (B-417)	swæsendum	red	ær	leste
	swæ (5X)	eðelred	ærist	mest
	ðær	medwe	ðære	gerece
	swę		ðæm	ðere
*859X870 (B-404)		meihand		enig
		sue (3X)		neniggra
		were		er
		meghond		mest
				ðem
				boem[11]
859 (B-403)		awege		ðem (2X)
		mege		elce (2X)
		sue		egwylce
		gere (2X)		
859 (B-497)		-med		
		medum (2X)		
		stret- (2X)		
868 (B-519)		mege	sęlen	

[11] This spelling is indicative of a confusion resulting from the merger of /æ/ and /œ/ under /ɛ/.

To these charters should be added the following two documents whose language is more obviously Mercian:

	$\bar{æ}^1$		$\bar{æ}^2$	
	æ	e	æ	e
*844X8455 (B-452)		ece (3X)[12]	aenig	
		werun	aerist	
			ðæm (2X)	
			ðaere	
*873 (B-536)	lẹne	meg-		
		(4X)	ðære	lestan
		foresprec	ẹrestan	þem
		swe (2X)	clẹnnise	
			gedẹle	
			ẹghwelc- (3X)	
			gelẹstan	
			ðẹm	

The first of the "Kentish" charters, with its single form of $\bar{æ}^1$ written e, may well be an indication of early raising in Kent. Even though it is a single form, it cannot be ignored. It should be noted, however, that the force of the data from the Kentish-Mercian documents points to a Kentish resistance to Mercian raising, especially since the data from the glossaries indicate that the Mercian raising of $\bar{æ}^1$ was complete by A.D. 700. The forms for $\bar{æ}^2$ are particularly interesting. As the glossaries show no raising, the e forms must be taken as a Kentish influence. It is particularly important that B-318 (805X832), which is void of es in eight examples, is a document conveying land in Sussex (Mercian territory of long standing). In sharp contrast, B-330 (805X810), while showing marked Mercian orthographic influence, is a charter conveying land in Kent. Consequently, its mixture of raised and unraised $\bar{æ}^2$s is not surprising. Badanoth's will, B-417, can be nothing but Kentish. The state of the language, complete confusion of $\bar{æ}$ and $\bar{e}$, is indicative of a scribe for whom there has been absolute neutralization but who is also familiar with

---

[12] The form ece is found in all dialects.

speakers who variously represent the two sounds. With the decline of Mercian authority, *e* becomes the exclusive graph for both sounds, as in B-404, B-403, and B-497. The same pattern is evident in the Mercian charters B-452 and B-536, both of which contain clear examples of Mercian letter forms. Berhtwulf's grant of land in Buckinghamshire (B-452) has the expected Mercian developments; whereas B-536, a grant of land in Kent, shows general Mercian developments with considerable numbers of exceptions. Mercian spellings are a function of Mercian political influence.

Given that Canterbury continued throughout the Anglo-Saxon period to be the major religious influence in the south, it follows that the whole speech community of Anglo-Saxon religious would be exposed to speakers who raised $\bar{æ}^2$. One is not surprised, then, to find $\bar{æ}^2$ written *e* sporadically in otherwise Mercian texts. The glosses in *Royal 2.A.20*, for example, have 17 examples of *æ*— *onæled* (3X), *ær*, *fæmnan*, *hæþan*, *hælend*, *hælende*, *hælo* (3X), *læde*, *þæm* (5X)—against 4 examples of *e*—*rerde*, *þere* (2X), and *þer*. It is worth noting here that individual lexical items are consistently spelled with either vowel but that there is no mixing within lexical items. The *Leyden Glossary* has 12 relevant forms. Five contain orthographic variants of *æ*: *gaesuopę* (for *gaesuępo*), *hlęderę*, *ymaeti*, *aenli*, *snędit*. The remaining 6 examples have *e*: *bleci* (2X), *heuuin*, -*suepe*, *snedil*, *agledde*. The exceptions are even more sporadic in the *Vespasian Psalter:* 13 *es*, 540 *æs* (written *ae* 270 times, *æ* 215 times, and *ę* 55 times).[13] From the perspective of lexical diffusion, it is worth noting that most of the exceptional *es* (11/13) are found in only three lexical items: *aledde* (3X), *enne* (4X), *flesc-* (4X). The *Bede Glosses* have eight examples, all with *æ; the Lorica Prayer,* two with *æ*.

THE DEVELOPMENTS OF GERMANIC *au*

Primitive Old English could derive two $\bar{æ}$ sounds from Germanic *au:* by i-umlaut ($\bar{æ}^3$) and by smoothing ($\bar{æ}^4$) of the normal [æə]

[13] The counts reported here come from Rudolf Zeuner, *Die Sprache des Kentischen Psalters (Vespasian A. 1)* (Halle: Max Niemeyer, 1881).

diphthongal development. The [æ] resulting from i-umlaut is con-
jectured on the basis of forms in Old Northumbrian. The Moore
Bede for example has approximately 45 examples, mostly with the
Æd- name element. The normal Mercian development was a sound
consistently written *e*. Unless *Corpus raedda* represents this development, the texts of this study exhibit *e* without variation.

There is, however, considerable and significant variation in the
representation of the smoothing product. The alternations in the
material common to the glossaries exhibit variation which can be
explained chronologically:

	ea	œ	e
Epinal:	*randbeag*	*læc*	*-egan*
	leag	*aecþan*	
	andleac	*hynnilaec*	
	teac	*garlęc*	
	fleah	*herebaecon*	
	geacaes		
	brodae leac		
	sigbeacn		
Erfurt:	*ondleac*	*læc*	*-lec*
	teag	*aec-*	*-lec*
	beanc	*gęc*	*-becen*
		ægan	*leccressae*
		rond baeg	*gecaes*
		læg	*-lec*
		randbæg	
Leyden:		*baeg*	*boeg*[14]
		gaeno	
Corpus:		*laec*	*-leec*
		aec-	*-becn*
		gaec	*egan*
		-laec	*ieces surae*

[14] A back-spelling resulting from the confusion of [ē] from both /œ̄/ and
/ǣ/.

The Developments of Germanic *au*

ea	*æ*	*e*
	-baeg	*sigebecn*
	laeg	
	onlaec	
	taeg	
	flęc	
	gęces	
	-laec	

Twelve additional *Corpus* glosses not shared with *Epinal–Erfurt* show a rather different development:

ea	*æ*	*e*
healecas	*taeg*	*tegum*
geac	*caecbora*	
	ynnilaec	
	waebtaeg	
	taeg	
	baeg	
	haehsedlum	
	haehnisse	
	herebæcun	

It is clear from these data that the smoothing of $\bar{æ}^4$ was not complete in the language of the *Epinal Glossary*. The fact that three texts agree on *læc* and *aecþan* is suggestive that the smoothing process had already begun in the language of the archetype. *Erfurt* clearly represents an intermediate stage on the way to the completion of the sound change as seen in *Corpus* and *Leyden*. There is no reason to posit underlying unsmoothed diphthongs for these last two scribes. Thus when the *Corpus* scribe met *healecas* (for *heah lecas*) and *geac*, apparently derived from a non-Anglian source, he did not reinterpret them according to a viable linguistically significant generalization in his own speech patterns. It may be further concluded, on the basis of his faithful representation of the unfamiliar diphthongs,

171

that the smoothing process was already complete in the language of his exemplar.

One can also see in these early data the beginnings of the sound change which would result in the normal Mercian development of Germanic *au/__χ. The *Omont Leaf,* the *Lorica Glosses,* the *Codex Aureus* inscription, and the glosses to *Royal 2.A.20* have exclusively *e*. The *Vespasian Psalter* shows the same development except for four examples of *þæh,* a weakly stressed word in which the further raising did not take place. At any rate, the glossary data can be restated in terms of the interaction of two variable rules. The first governs smoothing; the second, the further raising:

For *Epinal:*

$$\overline{æ}ə \rightarrow \langle \overline{æ} \rangle /\!\!\_\!\!\_ \langle \chi .40 \rangle$$
$$\overline{æ} \rightarrow \langle e \rangle /\!\!\_\!\!\_ \langle \chi .16 \rangle$$

For *Erfurt:*

$$\overline{æ}ə \rightarrow \langle æ \rangle /\!\!\_\!\!\_ \langle \chi .80 \rangle$$
$$\overline{æ} \rightarrow \langle e \rangle /\!\!\_\!\!\_ \langle \chi .45 \rangle$$

In both *Corpus* and *Leyden,* /æa/ has been restructured as /æ/. The same variable rule—probably coincidentally—accounts for the raising:

$$\overline{æ} \rightarrow \langle \overline{e} \rangle /\!\!\_\!\!\_ \langle \chi .33 \rangle$$

In the later Mercian texts (*Vespasian Psalter, Royal 2.A.20,* etc.), the *Corpus* raising is complete—/æ/ is restructured as /ē/. It is worth observing that two rules are required to account for the *Epinal* and *Erfurt* data and that they are crucially ordered in a feeding relationship.

As usual, one can count on the charters to provide data that run the full gamut of forms that might be expected in the Anglo-Saxon speech community. In the following listing, charters that concern grants outside the kingdom of Mercia proper (and thus were probably written outside Mercia even if by a scribe in the king's employ) are so marked.

The Developments of Germanic *au

		ea	æ	e
697	(B-97)			streteleg
759	(B-187)	uuisleag		(Gloucs.)
		godmundes		
798	(B-230)	leah		(Gloucs.)
*798	(B-289)	heaberhti		(Kent)
*803	(B-312)	aepelheah	aepelhæh	
		heahstan		
		heared		
		heahberht		
*805X810	(B-318)[15]	heagyðie	hęgyðe	(Kent)
			hægyðe	
*805X810	(B-330)		æc (5X)	(Kent)
808	(B-328)	heaberht		(Kent)
*811	(B-332)	heamund		(Kent)
		aeðelheah		
*811	(B-335)	aeðelheah		(Kent)
*812	(B-341)	eac		(Kent)
		aedelheah		
*822	(B-370)	heaberht		(Kent)
*825	(B-384)	wemblea	haeberht	
			baegswið	
*836	(B-416)	heaberht		
		croglea		
*844X845	(B-452)	heaberht	aec	
*873	(B-536)	eac (2X)	oferęcan	ec (Kent)
		beonheah		onfearnlege
		wulheah	horsalęge	
		beagstan		horsalege

Unfortunately, the data for $\bar{æ}^4$ in these documents is for the most part limited to place and personal names. Forms such as *heaberht, wemblea, heared, heamund,* etc. in which [χ] has been lost should probably not be considered counterevidence. That is, the change

$$\chi \rightarrow \emptyset$$

[15] Whereas *heagyðie* is the reading in *Stowe 7*, *hęgyðe* is found in the other extant MS of this charter—*Cotton Aug. ii. 100*.

bleeds smoothing. On the other hand, the vowel is not consistently smoothed even when the conditioning factor is present. The spellings tend to be conservative; even though Mercian orthographic influence is evident, non-Anglian forms predominate. A measure of Mercian influence in these documents is the extent to which non-Anglian names show the effects of smoothing. Any deviation is indicative of powerful Mercian influence. The data at least attest that Mercian scribes would be exposed to speakers for whom smoothing and raising did not occur.

SMOOTHING

The smoothing of Primitive Old English /ǣa/ has already been discussed in the context of the other sounds which passed through a stage of /ǣ/. The data, in summary form, is repeated here in a recapitulation of relevant forms containing /ǣa/, /ēo/, and /īo/.

eo

The diphthong [ɛə], which formed before -rC and [χ], was again monophthongized (smoothed) when C = [χ] or when it stood before [χ] alone. The smoothing process can be seen as nearly complete in the glossary data. The forms marked with an asterisk are glosses peculiar to the text in which they occur.

	e	*eo*
	/—χ	
Epinal:	þorgifect	
	suehoras	
Erfurt:	dorhgifecilae	
	sueoras	
	ceapnext	
Corpus:	þorhgefeht	
	sueoras	
	ceapcneht	

174

	e	*eo*
	l__ rχ	
Epinal:	berc	algiuu[eo]rc
	duerg	
	-uuerci	
	duuergaedostae	
	thuerhfyri	
Erfurt:	berc	
	duerg	
	uerci	
	duergae-	
	algiuerc	
	*bergas	
	*duerh	
Corpus:	berc	*licbeorg
	duerg	*briostbiorg
	werci	
	duerge-	
	þuerh	
	aalgewerc	
	*berc	
	*midferh	
	*baangeberg	
	*geberg	
	*duerc	
	l__ lχ	
Epinal:	elch (2X)	sceolhegi
Erfurt:	elch (2X)	sceolegi
Corpus:	elh	
	elch	
	scelege	

It is clear from these data that smoothing was complete before [χ] and nearly complete before [rχ] and [lχ]. The unsmoothed forms in *Corpus,* in glosses not occurring in *Epinal–Erfurt,* are perhaps to be discounted as deriving from non-Anglian sources. The form *briostbiorg* is particularly suspect as it contains the normal Kentish

175

confusion of /eo/ under /io/. As one would expect, smoothing is complete in the later Mercian texts (*Vespasian Psalter: weogum, steogum, spreocan*, etc. will be treated in what follows). Even in the charters, where forms are rare, the sound change appears to be complete:

*803	(B-312)	*bercue*	
		selesegi	
*805X807	(B-318)	*rehtlice*	(Kent)
*873	(B-536)	*reht-* (3X)	(Kent)

Smoothing is seen even in the two charters dealing with land in Kent, a factor elsewhere seen to inhibit the presence of Mercian forms. As the change is a general Anglian one rather than peculiarly Mercian, the added exposure to speakers affected by it may account for its penetration. It is important in this regard that the name element *-berht* appears almost without exception in charters of any provenience. While Campbell admits a change for /ǣa/ "reminiscent of Anglian smoothing"[16] in several "Kentish" charters, he switches his terminology to "palatal umlaut" when referring to the smoothed vowel of *-berht*.[17] He is silent on the matter in *Old English Grammar*.

ēo

This Primitive Old English diphthong, [e:ə], developed from Germanic **eu* and from the breaking of [ē]. There was in addition considerable early confusion of /ēo/ and /īo/, and either sound could be found in the smoothing environment. The following glosses are found in the *Epinal, Erfurt,* and *Corpus Glossaries:*

	eo	*e*
Epinal:	*cnioholaen*	
	buturfliogae	

---

[16] A. Campbell, "An Old English Will," *JEGP* 37 (1938): 149.
[17] Ibid., p. 150.

Smoothing

	eo	*e*
Erfurt:	cniolen	
	-fli[o]go	
	theoh	
Corpus:	cnioholen	-flege
		thegh
	*þeohsaex	*lehtfaet
		*flege

In sharp contrast to /eo/, /ēo/ is unsmoothed in *Epinal* or *Erfurt:* Both sets of glosses in *Corpus* exhibit the same tendency—a variable smoothing. Smoothing is complete in the slightly later *Omont Leaf*, *ðeh*, and *seles*.

The smoothing process was complete, however, by the time of the *Vespasian Psalter* which has *e* 12 times and *i* (by early confusion of /ēo/ and /īo/) 3 times. Examples are scarce in the other texts. They are sufficient to attest variation well into the Mercian period.

	eo	*e*
Royal Glosses:	leoh[t]	inlehtan
Lorica Prayer:		gece
Lorica Glosses:	ðeeoh	

io

Germanic /i/ when diphthongized (through breaking) produced Primitive Old English *iu* or *io*, probably [iǝ]. Although no forms with diphthongs attest breaking before [rχ] or [lχ], the existence of such forms as *iorre* suggests the more general change. Breaking before [χ] is abundantly attested as will be seen in what follows. The glossary data are representative of all Mercian texts except the charters. The monophthongization is complete; no *io*s are found (for economy, only the representative glosses in *Corpus* common to *Epinal–Erfurt* are cited here):

Epinal: frictrung, firgingaett, birciae, milciþ

177

Erfurt: frictung, firgin-, birciae, milcid
Corpus: frihtrung, firgen-, birce, milcit

Considerable variation is seen in the charters:

		i	*io*	
*742	(B-162)	*wihtredi*		(Kent)
*793	(B-274)		*uuiohtuni* (2X)	(Gloucs.)
*798	(B-289)		*wiohtun*	(Kent)
*801	(B-312)	*uuihtun*		
*805	(B-321)	*uuihthuni*		
*825	(B-384)	*wihtred*	*wiohtred*	
*831	(B-400)		*uueohtred*	(Middlesex)
*844X845	(B-452)	*owihte*		
		uuihthunus		

All of the charters with relevant forms also exhibit Mercian orthographic influence. In four of five examples, the unsmoothed vowel is found in documents with non-Anglian connections. The remaining form stands alongside a smoothed vowel.

īo

Examples of the Old English development of Germanic **iu* are rare; there are no data for the environment __χ. If Germanic /ī/ broke (and was subsequently smoothed) in this environment, the following glosses represent the development of this sound in the early glossaries:

Epinal: bitui[c]n, dislum
Erfurt: bituichn, dixlum, siid, *dixl
Corpus: bitun, þixlum, siid, *waegneþixl, *ðiendi, *bituihn

The form *betwih* is also found in the *Royal Glosses* and in the *Vespasian Psalter* (23X).

Smoothing

Chadwick has demonstrated that the loss of "interior -*h*-" was known in the language of the archetype of the glossaries.[18] As such *h* could be the conditioning factor for smoothing, interaction between the two sound changes is possible. In other words, the rule deleting [χ] would bleed smoothing. The universal smoothing in Anglian texts demonstrates that the nonbleeding ordering eventually won out. The data from the glossaries, in which both changes are synchronic with smoothing the further advanced, include examples of the residue which one expects to find in the case of two (or more) competing sound changes:

	æa	*eo* /__ *rχ*	*eo* /__ *lχ*	*ēo*
Epinal:	*steeli* *thuelan*	*suehoras*	*sceolhegi*	*cnioholaen*
Erfurt:	*steli* *thuelan*	*sueoras*	*sciolegi*	*cniolen*
Corpus:	*steli* *thuelan*	*sueoras*	*scelege*	*cnioholen*

The forms containing /æa/ can be discounted as they all occur before χi—an environment in which it is not at all clear that breaking ever occurred. The data provide five instances in which smoothing fails. The *Epinal* glosses all contain the conditioning factor, and the failure to smooth can be explained chronologically. The deletion of the velar spirant appears to have bled smoothing in the *Erfurt* examples, *sceolegi* and *cniolen*. If both rules are operative in the language of *Corpus* (one would like more examples), then they are crucially ordered in the nonbleeding relationship.

Anglian smoothing has long been documented, but an examination of the glossary data can refine our knowledge of it. In the following numerical summaries of the data, a plus sign is used to indicate that the process is complete; percentages indicate the progress toward completion. When the only nonsmoothed form is found in

---

[18] Chadwick, "Studies," pp. 229–232.

179

all three texts (and is therefore to be attributed to the conservative influence of the archetype), the change is considered complete. Such cases are marked with the plus sign and a percentage indicating the ratio of smoothed forms. For example, "+(95)" means that 1 example in 20 fails to exhibit smoothing and that that one example has parallel forms in the other glossary texts and is to be traced to the common archetype. The full data for /ĕo/ and /īo/ have been presented in this chapter, as have the data for /ǣa/. The data for /æa/ can be found on pages 135–140.

Smoothing before [χ]

	io	īo	eo	ēo	æa	ǣa
Epinal:	+	+	80	0	60	60
Erfurt:	+	+	+(90)	0	+(95)	80
Corpus:	+	+	+	+(66)	+(80)	+

Several observations are in order. Not only is it apparent that smoothing was complete by the time of *Corpus* and well progressed in *Epinal,* but the differences are, in addition, chronologically explainable. Such chronological differences have previously been noted but never quantified. Further, two general tendencies, of interest to natural phonologists, emerge. Short diphthongs were smoothed before the long ones. Among the short diphthongs, a hierarchy is to be observed: *io > eo > æa.* The resistance of /ēo/ to smoothing precludes such a statement for the long diphthongs.

Smoothing by Environment

A further breakdown of the data for the short diphthongs according to the environments is instructive. The smoothing of /io/, it has been noted, is complete in the early glossaries. The data for /eo/ and /æa/ may be tabulated as follows:

Velar Umlaut

	/eo/		/æa/		
	/__rχ, lχ	/__χ	/__rχ	/__χ	/__χi
Epinal:	60	+	30	60	+
Erfurt:	+(90)	+	+	+	+
Corpus:	+	+	55	+(90)	+

Again the *Epinal* glosses show the greatest resistance to smoothing. As i-umlaut significantly antedated smoothing, the variation due to the umlauting environment must reflect a process distinct from normal smoothing. The presence of a consonant between the vowel and the smoothing velar spirant slowed the process. In *Epinal*, and to a lesser degree in *Corpus*, the smoothing of /eo/ and /æa/ first begins before [χ]. The data, in fact, show a combination of the effects of environment and vowel height:

		/__Cχ	/__χ
Epinal:	/eo/	60	+
	/æa/	30	+
Corpus:	/eo/	+	+
	/æa/	55	+(90)

In *Corpus*, the sound change is nearly complete. The only vowel not completely smoothed is precisely what would be predicted on the basis of the variation observed in *Epinal*. This is strong evidence for the claim that the two texts represent the same variety of Old English at different stages of development.

VELAR UMLAUT

When /æ, e, i/ stood in the environment __CV$_{+back}$, the vowels were subject to a diphthongization known as velar (or back) umlaut. The data for the velar umlaut of /æ/ have been presented on pages 153–156.

5 Variation and Change in Mercian Old English

Except for the velar umlaut of the product of the second fronting of /a/ which occurs 70% of the time before a nonvelar consonant, the earliest glossaries fail to show evidence of the sound change. The only example in *Epinal* is *geolu* (*Erfurt geholu* is probably a scribal corruption of the same gloss). The sound change, on the other hand, is nearly complete in the *Corpus Glossary:*

/e/

feluspreci, elotr, treuteru, smero, sceraro, sceruru, eburðring, mettocas,[19] *lelodrae, belone, seto, wesan, onegseta smeoru* (2X), *smeoruul, tiorade, uueosule, ceonsol, beosu*[19] (2X), *sciopu, tiorade, ceosol, gefeotodne, feotod, feotur, feotor, seotu, seotul, meottoc,*[19] *meottucas,*[19] *meodolmlice, smeodoma, ðrifeoðor, creope, eoburthrote, eobor, eobotum, tuiheolore, steola* (2X), *heolor* (2X), *geolu* (2X), *feolufer* (2X), *feoluferð, eolene, eolone, freomo, weorod, teoru* (3X), *blaecteoru, speoru, smeoruwyrt*

/i/

pisanhosa, tigule, wituma, quiða, genung, rimo, smiton, hnitu seotol, glioda, ymbðriodung, lioð-, unlioþawacnis, nioðanweord, neoþouard, suiopum, suiopan, tioludun, uuiolocas, wiolucsel, wiolocreod (2X), *heorotherge, gionat, geonath, sionu, beheonan, sionuualt, cionecti, piose, piosan*

Both vowels /e, i/ undergo velar umlaut at the same overall rate (.75). There are differences when the data are broken down by environment:

	e	*i*	*æ*
/ __ labials	.85	1.00	1.00
/ __ sibilants	.80	1.00	1.00
/ __ resonants	.75	.85	1.00
/ __ dentals	.70	.65	1.00

[19] These examples may, as previously noted, contain the velar umlaut of [æ].

182

For both [ɛ] and [ɪ] the same hierarchy holds: labials > sibilants > resonants > dentals. The highest weighted environment is, of course, also one of the environments for which the sound change was most general in Old English. The lowest weighted environment was that environment in which velar umlaut developed in non-West Saxon dialects. It is further of note that velar umlaut began in the *Epinal–Erfurt Glossaries* with /æ/ and that the change is complete for /æ/ in the *Corpus Glossary* but still in progress for the higher vowels. The change is complete in the *Omont Leaf* (*beoloman, eofordrotan, eolone*), as one would expect because of the velar umlaut of [æ].

Velar umlaut was hindered in the *Epinal–Erfurt* material before [χ]. The same constraint is evident for *Corpus* for /e, i/; however, /æ/ is diphthongized to [æa] before the velar spirant. The relaxing of the constraint can also be seen in the *Vespasian Psalter* in which velar umlaut of all front vowels is the rule. The examples of diphthongs in the psalter are particularly interesting because they often occur by analogy when no back vowel is present:

> *asteogun* (2X)
> *bisweocun*
> *begreocu* (2X)
> *gebreaocendes*
> *gespreocu* (6X)
> *hreaca*
> *gesprecu*
> *spreocað* (13X)
> *spreocende* (7X)
> *spreocendra*
> *steorgun*
> *wegum* (26X)
> *weagas* (3X)
> *weogum*
> *wiðspreocen*
> *wreocu*
> *wreocende* (4X)

Although velar umlaut and smoothing were synchronic forces in the same texts, smoothing began earlier and was complete before velar umlaut. It is further advanced than velar umlaut in the *Epinal* and *Erfurt Glossaries*. Smoothing had ceased to be a productive force in the language of the *Corpus Glossary:* [æə] could develop before the velar spirant. It was obviously not a productive rule in the phonology of the *Vespasian Psalter* scribe.

The chronological difference observed between *Epinal–Erfurt* and *Corpus* can also be seen by comparing the development of velar umlaut in the early *Lorica Glosses* to that in the glosses to *Royal 2.A.20*. The sound change is variable but nearly complete in the former, complete in the latter:

Lorica:	*swiran* (2X)	*h[n]eofulan*
	onwlita	*toðreoma*
	smerun	*speoruliran*
		to teorenne
		feoluferð
		weolure
		heora
		daelniomende
Royal:		*heofenas*
		heofenos
		heofenum
		cweoðað
		siofeofoldlicum
		weorulde (3X)
		weoruld (5X)
		weolan

Since West Saxon influence was minimal in the early Anglo-Saxon religious communities, velar umlaut is the rule in the charters, as one expects.

*732	(B-162)	*freoðorne*
*803	(B-312)	*freoðuberht, freoðomund, freoðured*
*805X810	(B-330)	*feola, begeotan* (2X), *uuerolde, weorold-*

*836	(B-416)	*weodunman*
*844X5	(B-452)	*heofonum*
*873	(B-536)	`[ge]cweodu, gefeorum, begeotan` (2X), *heofones, weorld-*

The velar umlaut of /e, i/ is seen scattered throughout the charters in much the same way as forms deriving from an underlying /æ/. In B-312 and B-330, *ea* forms co-occur with *eo* forms. Such forms are peculiarly Mercian, although they may, for a short time, have been shared by Kentish.

THE FALLING TOGETHER OF *eo* AND *io*

It is a feature of later Mercian Old English that /ēo/ and /īo/ from any source fell together under *eo*, and the sound change can be seen variably throughout the Mercian period. The data from the glossaries give important information about the earliest stages of the shift. *Epinal, Erfurt,* and *Corpus* share the following forms:

Epinal	Erfurt	Corpus
	eo	
feormat	*craeomad*	*feormat*
geornlice	*geonlic(et*	*geornlice*
ageorna	*aquorna*	*aqueorna*
eornęsti	*eornesti*	*eornisti*
sceolhegi	*sceolegi*	*scelege*
cnioholen	*cniolen*	*cnioholen*
uuandae-	*-uuerpe*	*-uueorpe*
uuiorpae		
	io	
gliu	*gliu*	*glio*
cleouuae	*cleuuui*	*clouue*
	ēo	
steupfaedaer	*staupfotar*	*steopfaeder*
treulesnis	*treulesnis*	*treuleasnis*

Epinal	Erfurt	Corpus
getreeudae	getr[e]udae	getreuuade
fleotas	fleutas	fleotas
spreotum	spreutum	spreotum
eborspreot	eborspreot	eoborspreot
ceol	ceol	ceol
hleor	hleor	hleor
steor	steor	steor
leoma	leoma	leoma
beouuas	beouuaes	beowes
beost	beoth	beost
hlaeodrindi	hleodentri	hleoþrendi
ansueop	ansueus	onsueop
huueolrad	hueolraat	hueolrad
eorisc	eorisc	eorisc
eorisc	eorisc	eorisc
cneorissa	cneorissae	cniorisse
sueor	sueor	sueor
snidtreo	snidtreu	sniðtreo
buturfligae	-fli[o]go	-flege
gitiungi	geti[o]ng[20]	getiunge
	īo	
biouuyrt	biuyrt	biowyrt
gihiodun	gaeadun	geeodun
flio	flio	flio
thriuuintri	triuumtri	ðriuuintri
burgleod	—	burgliod

The *Corpus Glossary* also contains the following items not found in *Epinal–Erfurt:*

> *eo: weorð-, uueorð-, eordreste, eorðmata, weorras, steort,*
> *heor, geornis, orfeormnisse, smeoruue, sneorde,*
> *suansteorra, ceorl, seolbonan, ceolbarloma, ceoldre,*
> *heordan, briostbiorg, tiorade, scriopu*

[20] Sweet transcribes this gloss *get[o]ing*. In the manuscript the *o* is written over the *i*. I see no reason to generate an exception and prefer the alternative reading *geti[o]ng.*

The Falling Together of *eo* and *io*

io: hiorde (2X), horshi[o]rdas, neoþouord, geonath, geongendi, biheonan, s[w]eotol

ēo: aseodenne, þeotun, steor, ceodas, ðeoscip, werðeode, steorroðor, cleot, uueodloc, þeohsaex, heopan, cneoriht, treo (3X), onreod, eorodman, greouue, getreuuade, treuteru, plumtreu, mundeu (2X), hreod, steopsunu, steopmoder, deortuun, beost, beodbollę, seobgendum, reost, hlior, getriowad, tionan, eriopungae, briost, cneoholen, cnioresse

īo: briosu (2X), hrioseð, burliod, unhiore, gestrion, hio, glio (2X), gliowe, niol, frioleta- (3X), heldiobul, geeodun, geeode

The *æo* spellings are probably based on the confusion between *æ* and *e*, the first element of the *ea* and *eo* diphthongs. Both *Epinal* and *Erfurt* have spellings for the long diphthongs which reflect the Germanic **eu* and **iu*. *Erfurt*'s higher incidence of *eu*, for example, is to be explained in the scribe's attempts at faithfulness to an archaic exemplar which he did not understand. In the following summary of data, *eu* spellings are included under the counts for *eo; iu* spellings are included under the counts for *io:*

	/ēo/		/īo/		/eo/		/io/	
	eo	*io*	*eo*	*io*	*eo*	*io*	*eo*	*io*
Epinal	20	3	1	4	5	2	1	1
Erfurt	19	3	0	4	4	2	1	1
Corpus[EE]	20	3	1	4	5	1	0	1
Corpus	33	5	2	15	17	3	5	3

The scribes of these early texts had little difficulty keeping the long diphthongs apart. The data are amazingly accurate, especially considering that comparative data from modern and ancient Germanic languages attest widespread confusion. The variation in the data is concentrated in the short diphthongs: The *Epinal* scribe obviously could not tell them apart; the data for the glosses peculiar to *Corpus* indicates that the [ɪə] and [ɛə] from velar umlaut had fallen together under [ɛə]. The *Corpus* scribe consistently keeps the breaking diph-thongs apart, but [ɪə] from the velar umlaut of /i/ is spelled *eo* in all five occurrences and [ɛə] from velar umlaut of /e/ is spelled *io* twice, accounting for two of the three *io* back-spellings for [ɛə]. The sounds represented by the digraphs *ēo* and *z̄o* have completely merged in the *Omont Leaf*—*cnīo* for *cnēo*, *meoðo* for *mioðo*, *peopor* for *piopor*.

The material from the *Royal* glosses also attests the beginning of the merger under [ɛə]. The [ɛə] from breaking and from velar umlaut is spelled *eo: eorþan, heorte, heortan, mildheortnisse* (4X), *heofenas, heofenos, cweoðað, weoruld* (5X), etc. The [ɪə] from /i/ is kept separate—*siofen-*. The spelling *eo* is always used for /ēo/: *cneorissa, leoh[t], neosian,*[21] *feond-* (3X). There are mixed spellings for /īo/: *deofle, gefreode, hio* (2X).

Data from the charters are scant, but they show indications of confusion:

	eo	
*805X807 (B-318)	*geleornie, seolfa, geweorðe,* BUT *wiarð*
*812 (B-341)	*sueord*
*844X845 (B-452)	*siollanne*
*873 (B-536)	*feorm, weorld-* (2X), *weorðeð,* BUT *siolfne*
	io	
*844X845 (B-452)	*wudotunne, wotona*[22]
*873 (B-536)	*gewriotu* (2X), *geweoton* (2X), *weotum*
	ēo	
*805X807 (B-318)	*prioste, priost, reogol* (2X)
*805X810 (B-330)	*bebeode* (3X), *gebeode*
*844X845 (B-452)	*-beodon, bibeodoð*
*873 (B-536)	*leofust, geteod*

The confusion is complete by the time of the *Vespasian Psalter*.

---

[21] The vowel of *neosian* may come from Germanic **iu*. Old Saxon has *niuson* but Old Norse has *njosn*.

[22] See Campbell, *Grammar*, p. 89 on such forms.

188

The Falling Together of *eo* and *io*

The short diphthongs have been reanalyzed as /eo/. Kuhn's statement summarizes the situation:

> The evidence of the Psalter indicates that the diphthongs *eo* and *io* (from breaking and velar-umlaut of *e* and *i*) had fallen together in the dialect of that text [the *Vespasian Psalter*], and likewise the diphthongs *ēo* and *īo* (from West Germanic *eu–eo* and *iu*). The spelling *io* for the short diphthong is rare. The spelling *io* is still common, but it is frequently used in words, which, etymologically, should have *eo*, and *eo* is frequent in words which should have *io*.[23]

A look at the distribution of forms of words in the *Vespasian Psalter* derived from Germanic **iu* and **eu/eo* is instructive. The words in the following list are of certain etymology. Those listed under Germanic **eu* have attested forms containing Old High German *īo*, Old Saxon *īo*, Old Icelandic *jo*, or Middle High German *ie*. Those under Germanic **iu* have corresponding cognate forms with Old High German *iu*, Old Saxon *iu*, Old Icelandic *iu*, or Middle High German *iu*. From Germanic **eu:*

	io	eo
biod	1	4
ðeod	53	41
hreod	0	1
hleoðian	0	9
ðeof	0	1
leof	1	2
liomu	1	0
teonu	1	1
deope	0	1
asteopte	0	1
wilddeor	0	9
deorwyrðe	0	3
steoran	0	2
breost	0	3

[23] Sherman M. Kuhn, "The Dialect of the Corpus Glossary," *PMLA* 54 (1939): 10.

	io	eo
abreotan	0	4
ðeotena	0	1
cneo	0	1
treo	0	10
hweol	1	1

Of these 19 items, 13 have *eo* invariably; one has only *io; the balances vary between eo and io*, with *io* being written from 20 to 60% of the time. Why would a scribe write *hleodian, wilddeor,* and *treo* correctly over nine times each and fluctuate so dramatically over *ðeod?* Obviously he was insecure about the vowel in one-fourth of these lexical items while being certain of the vowel in two-thirds of the cases. The reason for his uncertainty can be seen in the data from words containing Germanic **iu:*

	io	eo
lordleod	0	5
ðiow	39	19
ðeostre	1	6
neosian	3	24
ðiowdom	1	1
ðiowian	6	1
eow	0	31
hreowsian	0	2
niow-	7	4
getreowan	0	24

In only one instance (and this word occurs only once) do any of these words contain only the etymologically expected vowel. For one-third of the lexical subset, the vowel has been reinterpreted to contain /eo/. The balance of the items show the sound change variously developed. The data for Germanic **iu* and **eu* are particularly important because they so clearly point to lexical diffusion. That is, /īo/ is not shifting as a phonetic entity to /ēo/, but rather the sound change is diffusing through the lexicon word by word.

190

The sound change has hardly begun for *ðiowian* but is complete for *getreowian*.

Lexical diffusion can also be seen at work with the short diphthongs /eo/ and /io/. The effects are the more dramatic because the sound change is all but complete. Only three words of all those which might contain [io] from breaking or velar umlaut of /i/ fail to demonstrate a completed change: *uðwiotun, uðweotun; ondwleota-* (18X), *ondwlita-* (5X), *ondwleata-* (2X); *nioðeran* (3X). In all three cases the diphthong is the result of velar umlaut of /i/.

THE UNROUNDING OF /œ̆/

Germanic /ŏ/ in i-umlaut positions became /œ̆/ in Old English; the front round vowel was spelled *oe*, occasionally *eo*. Short [œ] was rare because proto-Germanic **u* did not become **o* before /i, j/. Consequently, [œ] could form only in words in which a borrowed or analogical /o/ was found in the conditioning environment for i-umlaut. Both long and short *œ* had been unrounded to *e* in non-Mercian dialects by about A.D. 900. The round vowels remained the longest in Mercia, with /œ̆/ still prominent in the *Vespasian Psalter*.

Unrounding of /œ/ is not to be found in the earliest glossaries. *Epinal* has *loerge* and *soer[g]ęndi; Erfurt* has *coerin, loergae, sorgendi. Corpus*, however, presents quite a different picture:

œ	œ	e
coerin	caerin	cecil
sorgendi	laergae	deppentende
ðro[e]htig		
oemsetinne		

The *œ* spellings are to be taken as hypercorrections resulting from the development of both *œ* and *œ* to *e*. A full half of the data, then,

191

attest the unrounding. The vowel is consistently unrounded in the *Omont Leaf*, *foet* (5X) and *oele*.

Of the minor texts, only the *Blickling Psalter* offers any data containing /œ/. Its one example, *eletri[o]w*, has the unrounded vowel. The data from the *Vespasian Psalter* give evidence of a well-advanced sound change clearly proceeding word by word through the lexicon:

œ	e
oexen (2X)	*recetung*
doehter (2X)	*ele* (10X)
	eletreow (3X)

The unrounding of /œ̄/ proceeded at a much slower pace. Although examples are found earlier in the glossaries (*Erfurt* has two unrounded vowels out of 29 glosses—*beccae* and *gefegnessi*), the incidence in *Corpus* is significantly lower than for the short vowel: *ondest* and *sueg* out of 56 examples.

The minor texts give scattered examples of both the rounded and unrounded vowels:

	œ	e
Codex Aureus:	*beoc*[24] (2X)	*bec*
Blickling Psalter:	*adoen*	*guemde*
		onhrernisse
Lorica Prayer:	*boenun*	
	gedoeð	
Lorica Gloss:	*toeð*	
Royal Glosses:		*demdon*
		fet

Unless the *Vespasian Psalter* glosses containing forms of *bledsian* and *bledsung* exhibit an unrounded /œ̄/ (and it seems unlikely), the *Psalter* data fairly consistently show a rounded vowel. There are forms which apparently show at least a tendency toward unrounding.

---

[24] Apparently, *eo* became an orthographic variant of [œ].

The Unrounding of /œ̄/

Although the *e* spellings comprise less than 5% of the data, given the accuracy of the *Psalter* scribe one is reluctant to call them scribal errors. It should be noted that /œ̄/ is as often spelled *o* as it is spelled *e*. The data may mask a more advanced sound change; in at least three glosses, the scribe has corrected himself in an "error" and added the "dropped" *o: gedr[o]efde, hoene*,[25] *sw[o]etnisse*. At any rate, the Mercian data taken as a whole indicate that /œ/ unrounded before /œ̄/.

---

[25] Sweet reports this form as *hwene,* but Kuhn is correct in reading an *o* written over an erased *w*.

6

THE STUDY OF
EARLY OLD ENGLISH
SOUND CHANGE
IN PROGRESS

OLITICAL circumstances dominated the scene at the time of the production of earliest texts. Those texts were written by a politically sensitive social elite who employed the foreign (Latin) alphabet in which they were literate to transcribe the sounds of their own language. The first acts of vernacular literacy not only were concurrent with the rise of Mercian power, they were also the political records of Mercian kings or the products of religious houses supported by or under the influence of Mercian kings. Certainly we cannot know the exact geographical provenience of most manuscripts or the home (and native spoken dialect) of the scribes who wrote them. Even if we could localize the texts precisely, we would still need to meet the objections which Sisam raised to an overelaborated dialect geography for early Anglo-Saxon England:

> To avoid misunderstanding, the vagueness of our knowledge of dialect geography must be appreciated. Mercia—the Midland kingdom—was not divided from the West Saxon kingdom by a deterrent physical boundary, or even by a political line that remained fixed for centuries. In the late eighth century Mercian political influence was strong in Kent and in Wessex. In Alfred's reign Mercian literary influence was strong. In the tenth century Wessex dominated Mercia. These conditions are against well-defined dialect boundaries.[1]

On the other hand, we do have a good notion of the date of composition and hence the political provenience of the earliest texts. They are the products of Mercian Anglo-Saxon England. The documents that survive reflect linguistic, political, cultural, and social facts about Anglo-Saxon life; it is unproductively reductionist to

[1] Kenneth Sisam, *Studies in the History of Old English Literature* (Oxford: Oxford University Press, 1953), p. 95.

treat the texts monogenically as either linguistic or political or cultural or social in their origins. Thus, the linguistic features of the texts cannot simply be taken as features of a regional or historical variety. They are the features of a regional, historical, political, cultural, and social variety. Further, the language of the first English texts is a *written* variety. At first, that written variety was clearly a close representation of a scribe's speech patterns, but in the *Vespasian Psalter* we find the kind of regularity that suggests conventionalized spellings and standardization. The first standard variety of written English was a political variety based on the speech patterns of Mercian overlords. One critically important fact is clear: From the beginning, writing the English language has been a political act.

No field linguist would be surprised to learn that the earliest English texts reflect the kind of extensive heterogeneity recorded in the previous three chapters. First of all, that heterogeneity does not pervade the linguistic system; systematic contrasts and conditioned alternations are represented with the expected regularity. Further, the allophonic variations we do find are just the features which distinguished between major speech communities and historical (early Old English and late Old English) varieties. Most importantly, the heterogeneity is not a random admixture of forms; distinct patterns emerge from close study. Since the study of suballophonic, linguistically significant patterning in heterogeneous data is a recent development, one is not surprised to discover that a remarkable asymmetry exists between the rigid traditional view of early English dialects and the nature of the data found in the earliest texts. The purpose of this chapter is to begin to redress that asymmetry by proposing that early English textual heterogeneity reflects ongoing processes of early Old English sound change.

VARIATION IN THE MERCIAN
SPEECH COMMUNITY

Philologists have long noted that no two single early texts exhibit the same phonological system. While emphasizing differences between

197

MSS, English historical linguists have generally failed to notice some very important similarities. Several general observations can be made from examining Table 6.1, which provides a summary of synchronically variable data taken from the four major texts which span the period of Mercian hegemony. In the first place, much of the variation between the earliest texts can be explained chronologically. The steady progression of these sound changes toward the language of the *Psalter* emphasizes their close relatedness. The agreement between the texts is even more impressive when we realize that we have merely four informants from a highly diverse

TABLE 6.1
Chronological Summary of Sound Changes

	Epinal A.D. 700	*Erfurt* A.D. 750	*Corpus* A.D. 800	*VP* A.D. 825
Smoothing of *io*	+	+	+	+
Smoothing of *īo*	+	+	+	+
Gmc. *ǣ* to *ē*	.8	.9	.9	+
Smoothing of *eo*	.8	.9	+	+
Smoothing of *æa*	.6	+	+	+
Smoothing of *ǣa*	.6	.8	+	+
Smoothing of *ēo*	0/2	0/3	.7	+
Prim. OE *a* to *æ*	.3	.3	.3	+
Velar umlaut of *æ*	.5	.5	.8	+
io to *eo*	.5[h]	.5[h]	.6[h]	+
æ/__N to *e*	.3	.3	.9	+
Second fronting *æ* to *e*	.2	.4	.2	+
īo to *ēo*	.2[h]	0[h]	.2[h]	+
a/__N to *o*	0	.5	.7	+
Velar umlaut of *i*, *e*	0	0	.8	+
Unrounding of [œ]	0	0	.5	.7

a A superscript *h* marks cases in which a high incidence of hypercorrections suggests that the sound change has advanced farther than the percentage would indicate.

198

linguistic population. These data clearly reflect the wavelike diffusion of linguistic habits throughout the Mercian political community. The high degree with which the texts show the same implicational relationship between the progress of individual changes would be very surprising if these were texts of "mixed dialect." On the other hand, the close parallels argue that we are observing the same variety of the language at different chronological stages. As we move from this kind of overview treatment of sound changes to the more detailed study of the individual developments, similarities between texts become even more striking. The extended analyses of the various smoothing environments (pp. 174–181) and differing nasal environments (pp. 100–107) demonstrated that the same variable rules account for the data taken from all three early glossaries. Such consistency cannot be the product of scribal confusion and uncertainty.

Thus, the *Epinal Glossary*, the *Erfurt Glossary*, the *Corpus Glossary*, and the *Vespasian Psalter* form a continuum against which the remaining texts of this study may be viewed. Table 6.2, arranged roughly chronologically from left to right, summarizes the developments in the *Minora* of the sound changes which are synchronic in the early texts. Actual counts are given in those cases for which few examples are available. The data from these sources are, of course, extremely scant, and there are large gaps in this table. They do, however, offer a glimpse into an otherwise unrecorded period. Of these texts, the *Blickling Psalter*, the *Lorica Prayer*, and the *Royal* glosses do not depart from the language of the *Vespasian Psalter*. As both the *Lorica Prayer* and the *Royal* glosses derive from central Mercian MSS, their common language argues for a westerly provenience of the scribe of the *Vespasian Psalter* gloss. The only other clearly localizable text is the *Codex Aureus* inscription; it shows the variety of Mercian Old English to have been found in Essex. The *Leyden Glossary* is Germanized corruption of the continental glossary tradition best preserved in the *Epinal* and *Erfurt Glossaries*. The remaining texts, to varying degrees, exhibit some of the changes that are synchronic in the major Mercian texts. Because of the very nature of Mercian political control (overlords

TABLE 6.2
Sound Changes in the Minor Texts

	Blick. Psltr.	Leyden Gloss	Lorica Gloss	Lorica Prayer	Bede Gloss	Codex Aur.	Royal Gloss	Omont Leaf
Smoothing								
of *io*	—	+	—	—	—	+	+	—
of *ī̄o*	—	—	—	—	—	—	—	—
of *eo*	—	+	+	—	+	—	+	—
of *æa*	—	+	—	—	—	+	+	+
of *ǣa*	—	+	+	—	+	+	+	—
of *ēo*	—	—	(0/2)	(1/1)	—	—	(1/2)	+
Gmc. *ǣ* to *ē*	—	+	—	—	+	—	0	+
Velar umlaut of *æ*	—	0	+	+	+	+	+	+
io to *eo*	—	0	+	+	—	+	+	+
æ/_N to *e*	—	+	—	+	—	+	—	0
Second fronting	(1/2)	0.6	0	1/1	+	—	+	0
ī̄o to *ēo*	—	0	0	+	+	0	+	+
a/_N to *o*	+	0.7	+	+	+	+	+	+
Velar umlaut of *i, e*	—	—	0.7	+	+	—	+	+
æ to *e*	+	—	—	—	—	—	—	0
ǣ to *ē*	(2/3)	—	(0/1)	(0/2)	—	(1/3)	+(2/2)	—

ruling subkings), one would not expect to find total diffusion of Mercian speech characteristics throughout all of England. It is certainly telling that Mercian features are most heavily concentrated in western MSS.

R. M. Wilson, while agreeing that the *Psalter* (and its related texts) "shows no distinctively Northumbrian, Kentish, or West Saxon forms," claims "it does not follow from this that it must be Mercian."[2] For him, our knowledge of early Old English dialects is too limited to make any such designation. The texts, he argues, cannot be precisely located and might be from East Anglia, Essex, or Sussex rather than from Mercia. His argument fails on several points. First, even if the texts did originate outside of Mercia proper, they were certainly produced during the period of Mercian political ascendancy. The presence of Mercian letter forms and linguistic forms in Kentish charters of this period has been abundantly documented in this study. Further, Wilson rejects the term "Mercian" because he expects there to be only one variety of Mercian. He demands a linguistic homogeneity atypical of viable speech communities, especially communities that are joined by loose political bonds. If a text is non-Northumbrian, non-West Saxon, and non-Kentish, *and* written when Mercian kings were in control, it seems sensible to consider its language to represent part of the Mercian linguistic continuum. In addition, the language of the *Glossaries* and the *Vespasian Psalter* is closely related to that of the *Lorica Prayer* and the *Royal* glosses, which can be placed with reasonable probability in original Mercian territory. Because the occurrence of the same Mercian features rises and falls in the "Kentish" charters in a fashion that reflects Mercian political fortunes (further substantiated by Mercian orthographic influence), it seems reasonable to accept these texts as representative of heterogeneity in the Mercian speech community.

[2] R. M. Wilson, "Provenance of the Vespasian Psalter Gloss," in Peter Clemoes, ed., *The Anglo-Saxons*. (London: Bowes and Bowes, 1959), p. 293.

DATING THE EARLY SOUND CHANGES

Another consequence of this reinterpretation of early textual data is a need to reassess the standard view of Old English sound changes. Arguments for the probable chronology of those changes have traditionally been based on comparative analysis and reconstruction of Old English forms. Except for the work of H. M. Chadwick and Sherman M. Kuhn, scholars have all but ignored the evidence of manuscript variation. However, if one takes seriously orthographic variation, the received version of the chronology must be challenged. Old English scholars have proved slow to accept textually based arguments. Kuhn, for example, proffered convincing arguments for a rather late dating of the second fronting based on consistent variation in the early glossaries. C. J. E. Ball's response is typical:

> The small number of examples, the numerous corruptions, *and especially the fact that second fronting, though widespread, is by no means regular in these texts, all reduce the value of these forms as evidence* [emphasis added].[3]

Ball insisted upon equating regularity and analyzability, but A. Campbell appears to be unaware of the extent of variation in the earliest texts. After spending a lifetime studying Old English, he could still claim:

> It is accordingly not possible to date any of these sound-changes [including second fronting, velar umlaut, and smoothing] by observing their gradual appearance in texts, and we can establish their approximate dates and arrange them in chronological order by theoretical means only.[4]

Campbell then goes on to suggest the following probable chronological order of the changes, all of which he assumes to be prehistoric:

---

[3] C. J. E. Ball, "Mercian 'Second Fronting'," *Archivum Linguisticum* 14 (1962): 140.

[4] Campbell, *Grammar*, p. 106.

1. Anglo-Frisian development of nasal $\breve{\bar{a}}$; and of $\bar{æ}/\bar{e}$ from West Gmc. $\bar{a}$.
2. West Gmc. $ai > \bar{a}$.
3. Fronting of West Gmc. a to $æ$.
4. Breaking and the related processes of retraction.
5. Restoration of $\breve{\bar{a}}$ before back vowels.
6. Second fronting (mainly *VP*). Palatal diphthongization of front vowels, and early diphthongization of back vowels (mainly W-S and North).
7. i-mutation.
8. Smoothing.
9. Back mutation [velar umlaut].[5]

The variable manuscript data for the development of the nasalized a (item 1), the second fronting (6), smoothing (8), and velar umlaut (9) constitute the essence of Chapters 3–5 of this book. Is this not the "gradual appearance in texts" which Campbell demands? The balance of the changes in Campbell's list are indeed prehistoric. That is to say, they are represented without variation in the earliest texts. Not only do the textual data attest that second fronting came after i-umlaut, but Campbell's own argument for placing the second fronting before i-umlaut evaporates if one simply puts i-umlaut chronologically before second fronting:

> It would seem reasonable to assume that the analogical paradigm **faro, *faris, *fariþ*, which underlies W-S *fare, færst, færþ*, would be paralleled by **bero, *beris, *beriþ*. Since such a restoration of *e* is rarely traceable in many forms, an i-umlaut of *e* to *i* must be assumed for OE, to explain the prevailing absence of analogical forms with *e* where *i* stood in the following syllable. It would follow from this that the VP *e* from *æ* by second fronting was distinguished from *e* from Prim. Gmc. *e* till at least the time of umlaut, for the umlaut of the former is not *i* but *e*.[6]

The data for the i-umlaut product of West Germanic **a* before nasals argue, I think convincingly, for dating the raising to [ɔ] after

---

[5] Campbell, *Grammar*, p. 109.
[6] Campbell, *Grammar*, p. 76.

i-mutation. The umlaut product is variously represented *æ* or (raised) *e*. If the rounding had antedated umlaut, the resultant product would have been [œ] spelled *oe*, as was the umlaut product of [o]. Some will argue that the rounding of nasal *a* must have begun before fronting; otherwise /a/ before a nasal would have become [æ] as it did before all other consonants. This, however, is to confuse nasalization with rounding. The *Epinal Glossary*, for example, consistently attests the first fronting, but all examples (except one) of /a/ before nasals are written *a*. These data point to a nasalized but unrounded vowel. Forms such as Old English *fōn* require a little further explanation since it has generally been assumed that the rounding began before the prehistoric Germanic loss of *n*. In that way, a Germanic **fanhan* would become *fōn* through rounding then compensatory lengthening after the loss of the nasal. On the other hand, it seems just as likely that a long nasalized *a* might be raised to produce forms parallel to the normal Old English development of Germanic **ǣ* before nasals, which regularly became *ō* (*mōna*, "moon"; *ōm*, "rust"). There is evidence that Germanic **ǣ* passed through a stage of West Germanic **ā*, and it is certainly easier to understand how long *a*, rather than long *æ*, became *ō*.

The reasons for dating velar umlaut after smoothing have already been presented (pages 153–159). Second fronting, which is variably represented in the earliest texts, certainly postdates the nearly completed process of smoothing and would appear to have occurred about the same time as velar umlaut, though not as generally in early Old English. The revised chronology of sound changes then becomes:

1. Raising and rounding of Primitive Old English **ā* before nasals and the development of *ǣ/ē* from Germanic **ǣ*
2. The development of West Germanic **ai* to *ā*
3. The fronting of West Germanic **a* to *æ*
4. Breaking and the related processes of retraction
5. Restoration of *ă* before back vowels
6. i-mutation
7. Raising and rounding of *a* before nasals

8. Smoothing
9. Second fronting
10. Velar umlaut

Although an improvement on Campbell's chronology, such a statement can be further refined, as it still lumps together the various smoothing processes and claims a precise linear ordering of changes. Using *Epinal, Corpus,* and the *Vespasian Psalter* as touchstones, Table 6.3 more closely reflects the situation as attested by manuscript variation. The mixture of forms which we find in the glossaries, for example, can now profitably be explained as the residue of competing sound changes, rather than dismissed as "dialect mixture." As the sound changes become complete and solidified as processes in the phonological systems of Old English, we would expect the observed decline of such residue.

THE STUDY OF VARIATION IN MERCIAN OLD ENGLISH

The value of a variationist analysis of early Anglo-Saxon manuscript data goes beyond challenging traditional philological views about Old English phonology. Such work converges with contemporary attempts to study sound change in progress. Modern quantitative studies of language change offer a new methodology for historical linguists, while the extended study of 1200 years of nearly continuous data can provide a historical context of unusual depth for understanding contemporary change. The following summary discussion of the data of this book, then, simultaneously accomplishes two ends. First, it demonstrates that the variable manuscript data of this study are amenable to the same sort of analysis as modern data collected in their social settings. Second, it adds valuable historical evidence to the growing body of knowledge about the nature of sound change.

TABLE 6.3
The Chronology of Old English Sound Changes

	Epinal c. 700	*Corpus* c. 800	*Vespasian Psalter* c. 825
Smoothing of /io/			
Smoothing of /eo/			
Smoothing of /æa/			
Smoothing of /ǣa/			
Second fronting and velar umlaut			
Nasal influence of /a/			
Smoothing of *eo*			

The Study of Variation in Mercian Old English

The Transition Problem

The data of this study offer some information relevant to the questions of the regularity and gradualness of sound change. It is obvious from the discussions of synchronic variation within the body of this study that phonetic regularity is a factor in the development of sound changes. That is, we find classes of sounds undergoing changes for which a conditioning factor is often a phonetic environment. Phonetic classes, however, are not the only criterion. For example, the nasal *a* data from the Kentish glosses (page 96) and the *Vespasian Psalter* data for the change of *io* to *eo* (pages 185–191) strongly indicate that changes do not proceed uniformly by phonetic entity but diffuse through subsets of the lexicon. The changes can be seen as complete in some words while not yet having begun in others. These and the numerous other such examples (see Index) of this investigation suggest that lexical diffusion is a factor in many Old English sound changes.[7]

The data for many of the sound changes of this study have been reexpressed in terms of variable rules. Such expressions are more than convenient summary devices. By comparing the developments of sound changes at various stages of the language, we see that many of these changes were statistically gradual. That is, there were constraints on free variation, and the diachronic comparison of quantifications of variation indicates the direction in which the sound changes were progressing. Primitive Germanic *a* did not abruptly change to an [ɔ]-like sound (Chapter 3). The change to [ɔ] spread gradually by phonetic environment, beginning before [n] and last absorbing the environment of nasal homorganic consonant clusters. The sound changes studied here all attest that changes begin in limited and specific phonetic environments and spread gradually toward completion. That a single variable rule can account for variable data in several texts is a strong indication that the language varieties of those texts are closely related.

[7] For more examples, see Thomas E. Toon, "Lexical Diffusion in Old English," in *Papers from the Parasession on the Lexicon*, ed. Donka Farkas (Chicago: Chicago Linguistic Society, 1979), pp. 357–364.

6 The Study of Early Old English Sound Change in Progress

It is impossible on the basis of manuscript data to determine if Old English vowel developments were phonetically gradual or abrupt. One cannot know how many increments existed between [æ] and [ɛ] in the course of second fronting, increments masked under the *æ* and *e* graphs. Indeed, in several places the data suggest that perhaps subtly different pronunciations could be masked under one spelling. Consider the data for the developments of $\bar{æ}^1$, $\bar{æ}^2$, $\bar{æ}^3$, and $\bar{æ}^4$. These four etymologically different sounds were spelled using only two letters, but $\bar{æ}^1$ and $\bar{æ}^2$ must have had slightly (but perceptually) different pronunciations. The early Mercian scribes regularly raised $\bar{æ}^1$ to [e] and never raised $\bar{æ}^2$ (pages 163–169). Scribes could not have known that these two sounds were etymologically distinct, and the sound changes were not triggered by a transparent conditioning environment—any surface vestige of the umlauting vowel was for the most part long gone.

The Constraints Problem

The evidence presented in this study is of considerable interest to the natural phonologist. Although linguistic theory cannot at the present predict the direction of change, scholars have come a long way in identifying some of the universal directions toward which languages tend. The tendencies seen in this investigation are of two general types involving unstable phonetic entities or volatile phonetic environments:

(1) In changes affecting long and short varieties of the same vowel, the short counterpart tends, in Old English, to be the first affected:

    (a) /io/ became /eo/ before the change of /īo/ to /ēo/ was complete (pages 185–190).

    (b) /œ/ became /ɛ/ before /œ̄/ became /ē/ (pages 191–193).

    (c) $æ^2$ (the i-umlaut of *a*) was raised to [ɛ] before $\bar{æ}^2$ was raised to [e:] (pages 133–135 and 166–169).

    (d) /io, eo, æa/ were smoothed before /īo, ēo, ǣa/ (pages 135–140 and 180–181). That short vowels are more susceptible to vowel harmony is a fact related to this general tendency. In this light, it is interesting to note that velar umlaut (a sort of vowel harmony) only affects short vowels in Old English.

The raising of $\bar{æ}^1$ to [e:] before the "second fronting" of [æ] runs counter to this general tendency.

(2) W. Dressler has noted that stressed vowels tend first to be nasalized,[8] and the data of Chapter 3 support this claim.

(3) The raising influence of a following nasal consonant has long been observed.[9] We have seen that [æ] from the i-umlaut of West Germanic *a before a nasal is among the first of the [æ]-sounds to be raised and is raised in all dialects of Old English (pages 133–135). The raising to [ɔ] of Germanic *a before a nasal follows this trend. This raising can, of course, be seen as the last stage of a chain shift which began in Germanic, had already affected Germanic /e/ and /o/, and had resulted in *niman* and *cuman* by Primitive Old English times. The Germanic (or Primitive Old English) change of *ā to [ō] before a nasal is paralleled in Middle High German.[10]

(4) Labov has pointed out that velar consonants tend to reduce peripherality of vowels.[11] The velar spirant certainly presents one of the most volatile environments of Old English.

The Embedding Problem

The evidence just presented would suggest that some phonological changes originate as low level phonetic processes. When such changes within a group of members of a speech community are noticed and

[8] Wolfgang Dressler, unpublished paper delivered at the First Phonologietagung in Vienna, 1970.

[9] On nasalization see especially L. Schourup, "A Cross-language Study of Vowel Nasalization," *Ohio State Working Papers in Linguistics* 15 (1973) and T. Lightner, "How and Why Does Nasalization Take Place," *Papers in Linguistics* 2.2 (1970).

[10] W. Walker Chambers and John Wilkie, *A Short History of the German Language* (London: Methuen, 1970).

[11] William Labov, M. Yaeger, and Richard Steiner, *A Quantitative Study of Sound Changes in Progress* (Philadelphia: U.S. Regional Survey, 1972), p. 80.

imitated by others, a sound change begins. It is difficult to determine precisely at what point changes of this nature may be considered to reflect alternations in the phonological structure of a language. The evidence of this study, and that of other studies of sound change in progress, suggests that human linguistic competence includes structured variability. Within the paradigm of generative phonology, such competence can be expressed by variable rules. The issue that remains open is that of the point at which variable rules cease to represent physiological constraints in performance and begin to reflect competence.

When a new rule is introduced as a productive element in a phonological system, it can potentially interact with other rules of the language. When second fronting became productive in Mercian, it produced a segment [æ] which was subject to another productive force in the language—velar umlaut. As all second fronted [æ]s underwent velar umlaut, second fronting is crucially ordered before velar umlaut. Kiparsky has suggested that such feeding orders are not language specific and need not be specified in the phonological description of a language.[12] In the interaction of retraction, breaking, and raising described on pages 123–141, retraction and breaking are mutually bleeding—the rules alter their common input, with each thus precluding the operation of the other. The two rules are crucially ordered and cannot be ordered on any universal principle. It is a significant observation about Mercian Old English that breaking bleeds retraction, but the reverse is true for Northumbrian Old English where retraction bleeds breaking.

A side issue of the embedding problem of critical interest to this study is the question of the relationship of the Mercian Old English orthographical system to its phonological system. Do scribes represent an autonomous phonemic level, a systematic phonemic level, or a phonetic level? As all of the variable data of this study must represent free variation or the output of optional or variable rules, the writing

---

[12] Paul Kiparsky, "Language universals and linguistic change," in *Universals in Linguistic Theory*, ed. E. Bach and R. Hames (New York: Holt, Rinehart and Winston, 1968), pp. 171–204.

system obviously does not correspond to either an autonomous or a systematic phonemic level. To make any sense of the data studied here, one must assume (or is it conclude?) that a scribe's habits are motivated by surface phonetic forms. Sherman M. Kuhn has made much the same observation couched in the terminology of autonomous phonemics:

> I agree with Hockett [578 (1959)] that any analysis of OE phonemes must account satisfactorily for scribal practices. To be more specific, I am certain that the OE writing system (or any other alphabet system used for a language before the invention of dictionaries) was roughly phonemic; otherwise it would have been like an elaborate cipher, unintelligible to anyone who did not possess a special key. I am equally certain that the graphemes were roughly phonetic; otherwise how would anyone identify the phonemes?[13]

Linguistic contrast is an important fact about how languages operate, and a writing system must be able to convey the important linguistically significant contrasts of its language. But linguistic significance does not reside exclusively in contrast, and scribes (unconsciously) recorded their phonetic habits.

The Actuation Riddle

Although we can usually come up with a plausible explanation of a change after the fact, linguists have not as yet been able to predict precisely when a possible change is going to occur. This generalization is, of course, particularly applicable to the slow, regular internal sort of change which is typical of language isolation. Change caused by external pressure is quite a different matter. Because of the loose political structure of early Anglo-Saxon England, early English dialects must have been in constant contact (and conflict). We saw evidence of the actuation of a linguistic innovation

[13] Sherman M. Kuhn, "On the Syllabic Phonemes of Old English," *Language* 37 (1961), p. 524n.

when examining the development of West Germanic *a before nasals as reflected in the extant original charters made in Kent. Because the change of *a* to *o* is demonstrably tied to Mercian political fortunes and is concomitant with the appearance of Mercian orthographic influence, we cannot dismiss the manuscript heterogeneity as mere dialect mixture. We can, on the other hand, reinterpret this structured variation as an intersection of two separate aspects of the actuation and implementation of a phonetic change: a perhaps natural tendency of a nasalized low vowel to rise (a possible change) and social and political pressure (a reason to change). Variable data have been dismissed as dialect mixture when the hows and whys of dialect mixture embody the essence of the implementation and actuation problems. Dialect mixture is precisely to socially propagated sound change what variation is to overall contrastive pattern and alternation. We will better understand linguistic change when we know the reasons and processes of linguistic borrowing—one kind of possible linguistic change.

This study has conjoined the quantitative methods of modern linguistics and the rich tradition of philological inquiry in the hope of extending our understanding of one of the first principles of linguistic science: Living languages change. The curiosity that impelled early philological investigation was the desire to understand the texts in which our ancient written monuments are recorded. It is entirely appropriate that a byproduct of this "new philology" is an expanded understanding of ourselves as text makers. For too long we have focused our attention exclusively on the language of the texts. When we begin to view the texts in context, we realize that English historical linguistics is the linguistics of literacy. Since A.D. 700 we have made use of written English, and one of those uses has from the beginning been the solidification and expansion of political and social structures. The impulse to do so has become as much a part of our Germanic linguistic heritage as the words with which we conduct our daily lives—*mother, father, sister, brother, live, love, breathe, eat, drink, dream, think, read, write, die.*

THE TECHNOLOGY OF THE INTELLECT

The first sections of this chapter dealt with one aspect of alphabetic literacy; the perspective was restricted to a view of writing only as a new medium for speech. Precisely because of its newness, those first attempts at vernacular literacy could provide a record of speech free of the masking effects of conventional spelling. But, of course, speech could not go unaffected by its translation into writing. Writing was not the *mere* inscription of speech; writing introduced uses of English that simply had not existed for Germanic oral culture. Through writing, language could be put to the more efficient service of a developing society.

The dissemination of the benefits of what Goody has called "the technology of the intellect" depended, as he and Watt point out, on the nature and social distribution of writing.[14] The alphabetic nature of a Latin-based vernacular literacy made the writing of English a relatively easy matter, a minor realignment of abstract symbols and phonetic correspondences. The form of letters would need some alteration. The grand spaciousness of Anglo-Saxon majuscule (see Figure 2.2, pages 74–75, a facsimile of the *Corpus Glossary*, the apex of grace in majuscule script) and English uncial (see Figure 2.3, page 81), a facsimile of the *Vespasian Psalter*, the Latin is written in perfectly executed uncials) would necessarily give way to the simpler, more compact pointed miniscule (as in the *Vespasian Psalter* gloss). Expanded use of literacy required scripts that could be executed with speed and that allowed more text per page. Still, the skills of a scribe and the preparation of vellum implied both an expensive industry and limited access to the medium. Education required leisure, teachers, books—all the things that only an efficient and well-endowed monastery could offer. Hence, democratic literacy was not possible for early Anglo-

---

[14] Jack Goody and Ian Watt, "The Consequences of Literacy," in Jack Goody, ed., *Literacy in Traditional Societies* (Cambridge: Cambridge University Press, 1968), pp. 34–35.

Saxon England, although it would soon become the dream of King Alfred the Great. Writing belonged to an oligoliterate few who could only afford to maintain the luxury with royal patronage. In fact, because of its extended uses, literacy was no longer a luxury. It had become an instrument of power. Once Offa established his own *scriptorium*, written English would take on a *form* that reflected the kings' vested interest in its *uses*. The English written in texts after Offa would be the king's English (or at least influenced by the linguistic and orthographic usage of his altar-thanes). The technology of the intellect in the service of a king would produce inscriptions of his power.

REFERENCES

Bailey, Charles-James N. *Variation and Linguistic Theory*. Arlington: Center for Applied Linguistics, 1974.

Bailey, Charles-James N. and Shuy, Roger, eds. *New Ways of Analyzing Variation in English*. Washington, D.C.: Georgetown University Press, 1973.

Ball, C. J. E. "Mercian 'Second Fronting'." *Archivum Linguisticum* (old series) 14 (1962): 130–145.

Bickerton, Derek. "Inherent Variability and Variable Rules." *Foundations of Language* 7 (1971): 457–492.

Birch, W. de Gray. *Cartularium Saxonicum*. London: Whiting, 1885–1889.

Brooke, George C. *English Coins*. London: Methuen and Co., 1950.

Brown, Edward Miles. *Die Sprache der Rushworth Glossen zum Evangelium Matthäus und der mercische Dialect (I. Vokale)*. Göttingen: W. Fr. Kästner, 1891.

Brown, Edward Miles. *The Language of the Rushworth Gloss to the Gospel of Matthew and the Mercian Dialect (Part II)*. Göttingen: W. Fr. Kaestner, 1892.

Bruck, Anthony, Fox, R. A., Lagaly, M. W., eds. *Natural Phonology*. Chicago: Chicago Linguistic Society, 1974.

Brunner, Karl. *Altenglische Grammatik nach der Angelsächsischen Grammatik von Eduard Sievers*. Tübingen: Max Niemeyer Verlag, 1965.

Brunner, Karl. "The Old English Vowel Phonemes." *English Studies* 34 (1955): 247–251.

Bryan, William Frank. *Studies in the Dialects of the Kentish Charters of the Old English Period*. Menasha: George Bant Publishing Company, 1915.

Bülbring, Karl D. *Altenglisches Elementarbuch*. Heidelberg: Carl Winter, 1902.

Campbell, A. *Old English Grammar*. Oxford: Oxford University Press, 1959.

Campbell, A. "An Old English Will." *Journal of English and Germanic Philologie* 37 (1938): 132–152.

References

Campbell, A. *Charters of Rochester*. Oxford: Oxford University Press, 1973.

Chadwick, H. M. "Studies in Old English." *Transactions of the Cambridge Philological Society* 4 (1894–1899): 85–265.

Chadwick, H. M. *The Origin of the English Nation*. Cambridge: Cambridge University Press, 1924.

Chatman, S. "The *a/æ* Opposition in Old English." *Word* 14 (1958): 224–236.

Cook, Stanley. "Language Change and the Emergence of an Urban Dialect in Utah." Ph.D. dissertation, University of Utah, 1969.

Cosijn, Peter Jakob. *Altwestsächsische Grammatik*. Haag: Martinus Nijhoff, 1888.

Cosijn, Peter Jakob. *Kürzefasste Altwestsächsische Grammatik*. Leiden: E. J. Brill, 1893.

Dahl, Ivar. *Substantival Inflexion in Early Old English*, Lund: Hakan Ohlsson, 1938.

Davies, Wendy, and Vierck, Hayo. "The Contexts of Tribal Hidage: Social Aggregates and Settlement Patterns." *Frühmittelalterliche Studien* 8 (1974): 223–293.

Dieter, Ferdinand. *Ueber Sprache und Mundart der ältesten englischen Denkmäler*. Göttingen: G. Calvör, 1885.

Dolley, R. H. M., ed. *Anglo-Saxon Coins*. London: Methuen and Co., 1961.

Dolley, R. H. M., ed. *Anglo-Saxon Pennies*. London: The Trustees of The British Museum, 1970.

Dornier, Ann. *Mercian Studies*. Leicester: Leicester University Press, 1977.

Dumville, David N. "The Anglian Collection of Royal Genealogies and Regnal Lists." *Anglo-Saxon England* 5 (1976): 23–50.

Dumville, David N. "Kingship, Genealogies and Regnal Lists." In *Early Medieval Kingship*, edited by P. H. Sawyer and I. N. Wood. Leeds: The School of History, 1977.

Dumville, David N. "Liturgical Drama and Panegyric Responsory from the Eighth Century?" *The Journal of Theological Studies*, New Series, 23.2 (1972): 374–406.

Fisher, D. J. V. *The Anglo-Saxon Age*. London: Longman, 1973.

Fullmer, Daniel H. "Generative Inflectional Morphology and Phonology of Mercian Old English." Ph.D. dissertation, University of Michigan, 1969.

Goody, Jack. *The Domestication of the Savage Mind*. Cambridge: Cambridge University Press, 1977.

Harmer, F. E. *Anglo-Saxon Writs*. Manchester: Manchester University Press, 1952.

217

References

Hart, Cyril. "The Tribal Hidage." *Transactions of the Royal Historical Society*, 5th Series, 21 (1971): 133–157.

Hessels, John H. *A Late Eighth-Century Latin–Anglo Saxon Glossary*. Cambridge: Cambridge University Press, 1906.

Hill, David. *An Atlas of Anglo-Saxon England*. Toronto: University of Toronto Press, 1981.

Hockett, C. "The Stressed Syllabics of Old English." *Language* 35 (1959): 575–597.

Hogg, R. M. "The Chronology and Status of Second Fronting." *Archivum Linguisticum* (new series) 8 (1977): 70–81.

Holthausen, F. *Altenglisches Etymologisches Wörterbuch*. Heidelberg: Carl Winter, 1963.

John, Eric. *Orbis Britanniae*. Leicester: Leicester University Press, 1966.

Keller, Wolfgang. *Angelsächsische Palaeographie*. Berlin: Mayer & Müller, 1906.

Ker, Neil R. "A Supplement to *Catalogue of Manuscripts Containing Anglo-Saxon.*" *Anglo-Saxon England* 5 (1976): 121–131.

Ker, Neil R. *Catalogue of Manuscripts Containing Anglo-Saxon*. Oxford: Oxford University Press, 1957.

Keyser, S. J. "Metathesis and Old English Phonology." *Linguistic Inquiry* 6 (1975): 377–411.

Kiparsky, Paul, and O'Neil, Wayne, "The Phonology of Old English Inflections," *Linguistic Inquiry* 7 (1976): 527–557.

Köhler, Theodor. *Die Altenglischen Namen in Baedas Historia Ecclesiastica*. Berlin: Mayer & Müller, 1908.

Kuhn, Sherman M. "*e* and *æ* in Farman's Glosses." *PMLA* 60 (1945): 631–669.

Kuhn, Sherman M. "On the Consonantal Phonemes of Old English." *Philological Essays: Studies in Old and Middle English Language and Literature in Honour of Herbert Dean Meritt*. 1967.

Kuhn, Sherman M. "On the Syllabic Phonemes of Old English." *Language*, 37 (1961): 522–538.

Kuhn, Sherman M. "The Dialect of the Corpus Glossary." *PMLA* 54 (1939): 1–19.

Kuhn, Sherman M. *The Vespasian Psalter*. Ann Arbor: University of Michigan Press, 1965.

Kuhn, Sherman M., and Quirk, R. "Some Recent Interpretations of Old English Digraph Spellings." *Language* 29 (1953): 143–156.

Kuhn, Sherman M., and Quirk, R. "The Old English Digraphs: A Reply." *Language* 31 (1955): 390–401.

Kurath, Hans. "The Binary Interpretation of English Vowels: A Critique." *Language* 33 (1957): 111–122.

References

Labov, William. "On the Use of the Present to Explain the Past." *Proceedings of the Eleventh International Congress of Linguists* 2 (1974): 825–851.

Labov, William. "Resolving the Neogrammarian Controversy." *Language* 57 (1981): 267–308.

Labov, William. *Sociolinguistic Patterns*. Philadelphia: University of Pennsylvania Press, 1972.

Labov, William, Yaeger, M., and Steiner, R. *A Quantitative Study of Sound Changes in Progress*. Philadelphia: The U.S. Regional Survey, 1972.

Lass, Roger. *On Explaining Language Change*. Cambridge: Cambridge University Press, 1980.

Lass, Roger. "Palatals and Umlaut in Old English." *Acta Linguistica Hafniensia* 1 (1970): 25–30.

Lass, Roger, and Anderson, J. H. *Old English Phonology*. Cambridge: Cambridge University Press, 1975.

Lindsay, W. M. *The Corpus Glossary*. Cambridge: Cambridge University Press, 1921.

Lowe, E. A. *Codices Latini Antiquiores*. Oxford: Oxford University Press, 1935.

Luick, Karl. *Historische Grammatik der Englischen Sprache*. Oxford: Basil Blackwell, 1964.

Meritt, Herbert Dean. *Old English Glosses (A Collection)*. New York: Kraus Reprint Company, 1971.

Miller, Thomas. *Place Names in the English Bede*. Strassburg: Karl J. Trübner, 1896.

Miller, Thomas. *The Old English Version of Bede's Ecclesiastical History of the English People*. London: Oxford University Press, 1890.

Moore, Samuel, Meech, Sanford B., and Whitehall, Harold. "Middle English Dialect Characteristics and Dialect Boundaries." *Essays and Studies in English and Comparative Literature*, 13. Ann Arbor: University of Michigan Press, 1935.

Pheifer, J. D. *Old English Glosses in the Epinal–Erfurt Glossary*. Oxford: Oxford University Press, 1974.

Robb, K. A. "Some Changes in Kentish Old English Phonology." *Lingua* 20 (1968): 177–186.

Sauer, Romauld. *Zur Sprache des Leidener Glossars*. Augsburg: Ph. Pfeiffer, 1917.

Sawyer, Peter H. *Anglo-Saxon Charters. An Annotated List and Bibliography*. London: Butler & Tanner, 1968.

Sawyer, Peter H. *From Roman Britain to Norman England*. New York: St. Martin's Press, 1978.

Sawyer, Peter H., and Wood, Ian N., eds. *Early Medieval Kingship*. Leeds: The School of History, 1977.

References

Schauman, Bella, and Cameron, Angus. "A Newly-found Leaf of Old English from Louvain." *Anglia: Zeitschrift für Englische Philologie* 95 (1977): 289–312.

Sievers, Eduard. *Angelsächsische Grammatik.* Halle: Max Niemeyer, 1898.

Sisam, Celia. "An Early Fragment of the *Old English Martyrology.*" *The Review of English Studies,* 4 N.S. (1953), p. 209.

Sisam, Kenneth. *Studies in the History of Old English Literature.* Oxford: Oxford University Press, 1953.

Sledd, James. "Some Questions of English Phonology." *Language* 34 (1958): 252–258.

Stenton, Dorothy, ed. *Preparatory to Anglo-Saxon England.* Oxford: Oxford University Press, 1970.

Stenton, F. M. *Anglo-Saxon England.* Oxford: Oxford University Press, 1943.

Stenton, F. M. *The Latin Charters of the Anglo-Saxon Period.* Oxford: Oxford University Press, 1955.

Stockwell, Robert. "The Phonology of Old English: A Structural Sketch." *Studies in Linguistics* 13 (1958): 13–24.

Stockwell, Robert, and Barritt, C. "Scribal Practice: Some Assumptions." *Language* 37 (1961): 75–82.

Stockwell, Robert, and Barritt, C. "Some Old English Graphemic–Phonetic Correspondences—*æ, ea,* and *a.*" *Studies in Linguistics: Occasional Papers* 4 (1951).

Stockwell, Robert, and Barritt, C. "The Old English Short Digraphs: Some Considerations." *Language* 30 (1954): 1–42.

Stockwell, Robert, and Willard, R. "Further Notes on Old English Phonology." *Studies in Linguistics* 14 (1959): 10–13.

Ström, Hilmer. *Old English Personal Names in Bede's History.* Lund: Hakan Ohlsson, 1939.

Sweet, Henry. *History of English Sounds.* Oxford: Oxford University Press, 1888.

Sweet, Henry, ed. *The Oldest English Texts.* Oxford: Oxford University Press, 1885.

Thompson, E. M. *An Introduction to Greek and Latin Palaeography.* Oxford: Oxford University Press, 1912.

Toon, Thomas E. "Lexical Diffusion in Old English." In *Papers from the Parasession on the Lexicon,* edited by Donka Farkas, Wesley M. Jacobsen, and Karol W. Todrys. Pp. 357–364. Chicago: Chicago Linguistic Society, 1979.

Vleeskruyer, R., ed. *The Life of St. Chad.* Amsterdam: North-Holland Publishing Company, 1953.

Wagner, K. *Generative Grammatical Studies in the Old English Language.* Heidelberg: Julius Gross, 1969.

References

Wang, William S.-Y. "Vowel Features, Paired Variables, and the English Vowel Shift." *Language* 44 (1968): 695–708.

Wang, William S.-Y. "Competing changes as a cause of residue." *Language* 45 (1969): 9–45.

Wang, William S.-Y., and Cheng, Chin-chuan. "Implementation of Phonological Change: The Shuand-feng Chinese Case." In *Papers from the Sixth Regional Meeting of the Chicago Linguistic Society*, pp. 552–559. Chicago: Chicago Linguistic Society, 1970.

Weinreich, Uriel, Labov, William, and Herzog, Marvin I. "Empirical Foundations for a Theory of Language Change." In Lehmann, W. P., and Malkiel, Yakov, *Directions for Historical Linguistics*. Austin: University of Texas Press, 1968.

Whitelock, Dorothy. *The Audience of Beowulf*. Oxford: Oxford University Press, 1951.

Whitelock, Dorothy, ed. *English Historical Documents c. 500–1042*. London: Eyre & Spottiswoode, 1955.

Wright, Joseph. *The English Dialect Grammar*. London: Oxford University Press, 1905.

Wright, Joseph, and Wright, Mary. *Old English Grammar*. Oxford: Oxford University Press, 1914.

Zeuner, Rudolf. *Die Sprache des Kentischen Psalters*. Halle: Max Niemeyer, 1881.

Zupitza, Julius. "Merchisches aus der Hs. Royal 2 A 20 im Britischen Museum." *Zeitschrift für Deutsches Alterthum* 33 (1889): 47–66.

INDEX

223

Index

Index

Index

Index

Index

Index

229